DRINKERS OF THE WIND

The Blue-Blood of Arabia
Wudiyeh, Rashayd's war mare,
was of this strain.

DRINKERS OF THE WIND

WIND *BY CARL R. RASWAN*

ARIEL BOOKS · NEW YORK

Ariel Books
a division of
Farrar, Straus and Cudahy

Published simultaneously in Canada by
Ambassador Books, Ltd., Toronto

Manufactured in the U. S. A.
By American Book-Stratford Press, Inc.

Contents

Phili — The Horse of My Boyhood   9

Ghazal — The Drinker of the Wind   25

Wudiyeh — War Mare of the Desert   67

The Homecoming of the Horses   127

Two of the illustrations appearing in this book are reproduced from the author's Black Tents of Arabia *by permission of the publishers, Little, Brown & Company.*

Phili—The Horse of My Boyhood

HE WAS AN impatient creature with quivering limbs. His eyes flashed fiery light. His nostrils flared defiance. He tossed his head up on a lofty neck. His carriage was noble and his shape handsome, set upon the most tender feet.

He hung in an old stained oaken frame above my bed. Phili, I called him, but my father called him Phalius, for the horse of Thessaly, who wore a white star on his forehead.

I loved Phili. I was only three when my father observed my unusual interest in horses. He read simple old Greek tales to me, and I became familiar with the horses of ancient Greek mythology. Not even horsemen understood expressions I used until Father came to the rescue.

One day at our county horseshow I thought that I had discovered the original Phili, a golden chestnut pony with a curly mane and an arched tail. I stared with envious eyes at the boy of ten who rode him. When I begged Father to buy him, he said that I must wait. Perhaps in two years he would begin to make a horseman of me.

Our house stood not far from the tree-shaded country road along which riders were allowed to pass. My eyes scarcely reached the level of the window sill, and I had to stand on tiptoe to watch the horses go by. One Sunday morning I heard two riders approach. The sound of hoofs was so resonant that I listened with bated breath. Phili, my white-starred Phili, had come. This was surely the hollow cymbal ring of his small hoofs as they struck the hard roadway. The noise of the other horse's feet was only the clatter of an ordinary animal.

I raced through the house, and out into the garden, as far as the fence, which at that time limited my world. Opposite me, two riders were passing our house. One of them was mounted on a dapple-grey, a small but powerful animal, playfully pawing the air with his forelegs as he danced over the road. His motions were effortless; his rider enjoyed them with reins slack and firm but easy seat. Steed and rider were such a picture of grace and the hollow ring of hoofs such music to my ears, that I have not forgotten it throughout my life. Nor have I forgotten the dark horse at his side, clumsily forging ahead—a spiritless creature.

Suddenly my father stood next to me. Without a word he lifted me to his shoulder and walked along parallel to the garden fence.

"This is an Arabian from Hungary," Father said. "The King has bought him for his royal stable."

I gazed after the Arabian horse, from my father's shoulders, until the animal disappeared under a big chestnut tree with pink candelabra of sweet blossoms.

I scrambled down his back; tears of chagrin filled my eyes. "Oh, Father!" I cried, "this horse is more beautiful than Phili!"

Father smiled. "Yes, he is. The Arabian is the king of all horses."

On my fifth birthday Father gave me the golden chestnut pony that I had seen two years earlier at the county fair. Now I had my Phili with the curly mane and the proud

10

head and dainty feet. He seemed to have descended from the picture on my wall, dashing into my young life to receive all my enthusiasm and affection.

Either the romantic spark of Hungarian blood, inherited from my mother, or the restless urge of the soul of Ulysses, the hero of my father's classic bedtime stories, tempted me to a daring escapade.

Not more than a quarter of a mile from our house flowed the Elbe River, with its hills beckoning from the other side. I told a neighbor's son, a boy of my age, that the world began behind those hills across the river, and that, if he had the courage, this little stretch of water would no longer keep us from seeing for ourselves how the whole world looked.

While the nurse was having her afternoon coffee, we hitched Phili to my baby sister's wicker-basket carriage, stowed the baby in it, and drove off—along the road to the Elbe and then into the river. We stood up to our knees in mud and water, with a dense jungle of reeds about us, and Phili and the carriage would not move further.

As the hours passed, we began to feel lonesome and forsaken. At last I heard people calling to each other, and suddenly men ran down to the river and hustled us out of the mud and brought us home.

Father asked me why I had done such a dreadful thing as to try to cross the river. I explained carefully, "I wanted to go beyond the hill, and see the world." And in the same breath I asked how far the world was beyond the hill.

"How far? Oh, far. Very far!" Father answered. "When you come to the top of the hill, there is another hill."

"And," I interrupted, "when you come to the other hill, you see the world?"

"No, there is another hill."

"And then you see the world?" I asked.

"No, of course not. It goes on and on—hill and plains, more plains and high mountains."

"But when do you see the world?" I persisted.

"This is the world," Father answered patiently. "Right where you stand, right under you. If you go on and on, you will only come back here to this place where you stand now."

Father held up his clenched hand. "You see this knuckle? This is the first hill, and these are other hills. Then comes big water and more land and hills. You would go all around them and come right back again to this little water, and to this same little hill."

After all, he was my father and he must be right. But somehow I still felt—and I believe I do to this day—that beyond the next hill, or the one after that, I shall come to see the world.

Two years after Phili came into my possession, I was allowed to sit down to the rudiments of practical horsemanship—to learn how to understand and guide Phili's animal intelligence.

I had little fear of horses. This was no virtue but an acquired talent. After the adventure in the river, I learned to give as much confidence to an animal as he gave to me. I was never allowed to punish him with blows, never to thrust my will upon him with force. We children were taught to reason with ourselves before we tried to reason with an animal, and thus remain the master. That was the secret.

Phili was about my own age. We had a language, and I talked to him practically all the time. I was sure that he understood. A smack of the lips, a kisslike, quickly repeated chirrup, would calm him down instantly, no matter how high his spirit. And just as quickly, I could snatch him from lethargy by clucking my tongue against the roof of my mouth. His spirit would be aroused at once, and, when I combined the clucking with a forward touch of my heels, he would bound away with me.

I was convinced that Phili was a horse for heroes and gods, and I treated him accordingly. He stood his honors well, though he was not more than twelve hands from his shining black hoofs to his small withers. He was a mettlesome fellow, I was warned; he has a temper like a man, they told me. But with a gentle hand and supreme childlike confidence I found him only exceedingly ambitious.

He could gallop as if animated by blind wrath. His dash at full speed was a task for a seven-year-old, and his controlled action in the show ring was breathtaking. But I handled him well enough after three months to be allowed to take him on the road in the company of other people, children and grownups.

But not everything was sheer, painless joy. I had to ride Phili bareback, with my legs dangling entirely free from the knees down. It takes some time before the muscles become supple, even in a child. But when Phili was urged by the master's whip to leap ahead, I was ordered to forget the hold with my legs and to take the sudden, heavy jolts by balancing and shifting my weight forward a little over the withers.

A quiet seat and the gentlest of hands were required, hands that inspired both confidence and obedience. But most important was a calm mental attitude. Our riding master stressed that there was no disorder except *within* us. It would not be found in the horse unless it had first been transmitted from the rider to the animal.

I learned to correct the faults of the horse in myself and

13

to watch him only for my own joy and delight in him. How proudly he would hold up his head, arch his neck, and glory in his own graceful action, lifting his legs freely and bearing his tail with style.

"Induce him to feel free—rouse his spirit to glory—soothe and calm him down with a quiet hand, and a cheerful chirrup." Those were the classic remarks of my old Rittmeister, a captain of cavalry.

"Never let his fire die out, but kindle it with words, and make him feel the joy that is within you; let him know that you are honored to be carried along on his strong shoulders and back and on his swift feet."

So the old riding master gave us an almost spiritual interpretation of the art of riding. Composure and tranquillity, he would repeat, were more vital than muscular action.

"It is as if you were centaurs," he would say, warming to his subject. "All the grace and precision of the animal are within you, and you become part of the complex creature. . . ."

Sometimes, when I rode Phili, I wanted to hold on to his long, curly mane. It was tempting, but I was told that the mane did not exist.

"You don't want Phili to prance about with a short, hogged mane? Your disgrace would be Phili's own disgrace."

Nothing could have hurt me more than that.

For jumping lessons a small, folded blanket was permitted. It was fastened by a girth under the belly of my pony, but I was never allowed to touch either one with my hand after I had swung my leg over Phili's back. I had to ride for miles with folded arms—walk, trot, and canter—and last, but not least, to jump with arms crossed, hands on my shoulders or thumbs in my belt.

14

And to attend to Phili, his feed and his stable, I had to get up at five o'clock in the morning.

The swift, happy years raced by. I was outgrowing Phili a little, but he still proved to be an excellent companion. I was deep in Latin and Greek, and life suddenly began to be very serious. It was not all play, I learned—not just what I could get, but what I could give, too.

There was a dual life developing within me. The one of reality and the other of dreams. The one of form and fact, and the other of intangibles. This conflict was the price I paid for beginning the study of Greek. However, much of the time my feet remained on the firm ground of reality; I swung them across the back of a horse and felt that the world was still round, and the sun was life to me.

Now I rode bareback a great deal because the ancient Greeks had done it. My horse was fed on barley instead of oats, on the advice of the ancients. From Pollux I learned to use warm water to wash the mouth of Phili, to anoint his hoof bars with pure olive oil, and to rub it into his skin and gums.

One day I rode Phili into the lake at the Moritzburg castle. I had read and reread in "Tyro" about the intelligent young mare who had recognized her own image in the meadow stream. Would Phili? This day I dared to test it. His semblance was perfect, as in a mirror, and there was not a ripple on the pool as he stood gazing for minutes at his own likeness. I saw that he recognized his image in the clear water.

From then on I called it "the pool of Sophocles" because Phili had had the noble spirit of the Greek mare of Sophocles. I took many other horses there, but they were all indifferent to their image. I called them stupid creatures.

15

One day Prince Ernst came riding on the Arabian stallion which his father had bought in Hungary years ago—the one I had seen prancing along the old country road. The horse was almost white with age, though he had been a dapple-grey.

Anxiously, I watched the Prince as he rode his horse into the pool, and I remembered my father's words, that above all, the Arab is the King of horses. I shall never forget when he splashed into the water. He recognized his image at once, though the disturbed water rippled, and the stallion's image trembled on the opal surface. It seemed animated with life, swaying back and forth, and the handsome steed played with his image, tossing his feet with light touches upon the surface of the pool, keeping the ripples vibrating, and enjoying the picture dancing so vividly before his eyes. I decided that the Arabian had greater intelligence than little Phili.

At that time I still thought that the ancient Greek horse was the acme of beauty and perfection, and that he had disappeared with the decline of the Athenian republic. Deeper and deeper I became engrossed in the Greek classics; more and more I began to identify myself with the spirit of Hellas. One thing amazed me—the smallness of the Greek horses. They seemed to be twelve to thirteen hands only, not much larger than Phili. Father, however, explained that the size of the ancient Greek horse was deceptive.

Greek friezes were placed in elevated positions, and thus, viewed from below, the figures of men and horses were brought into harmonious proportions. Whether mounted or walking, the human figure was always even with the highest point of the horse, and naturally this had to be accomplished by sacrificing the actual size and height of the animal and exaggerating the human figures.

16

So influenced were we by the games of the ancient Greeks that we developed the idea of hurling javelins against wicker targets nailed to posts at about the level of the riders' heads. This required a good deal of practice, and we played for weeks before we achieved enough skill to play the game according to the rules set down by the ancient writers on horsemanship. The skirmish, the wheeling about, the pressing on at full speed in order to be the first to return to the line of one's own riders—that was the thrill of the game.

One day, after watching our game, my riding master took me aside. "Do you see how the force that carries the spear through the air is your own?" he asked. "And the course it takes through space is the path of your calculating mind? Do you see that the animal under the control of your hands and legs is part of yourself? *You* speed the whirling hoofs; *you* turn the body of closely knit muscles and nerves. *You* are the animator of the javelin, *you* are the horse."

2

AT SEVENTEEN I had three years of Plato and Aristotle behind me. Aristotle had taught me that the evolutionary pattern of nature led to Plato's perfect form. The thought of the *perfect* creature haunted my heart. Loving horses as I did, I was filled with a deep certainty that there was an evolving pattern to the perfect horse. And while I still loved Phili, I was also aware that he had not stepped from the immortal frieze of the Parthenon! This little stab I was forced to suffer for having rubbed elbows a brief moment with the ancient world of Athens.

When I had finished my humanistic studies, I was promised my first vacation in Greece.

The people I met on the boat and the ever-changing sights on the shores of Europe and Asia fascinated me. Ancient walls and towers rose in the distance, and dark spirelike cypresses sprang from white marble slabs in Turkish cemeteries. Gigantic umbrella-like pines shaded white houses with uplifted crowns.

Stambul was another world, a world that I could not grasp in our short two-day stay. Hundreds of minarets pierced the blue sky. I saw the wide dome of St. Sophia, the Seraglio, and the tombs of the Sultans; the Island of Prinkipo, the Golden

Horn, the tower of Pera. . . . Happy, bewildered, and exhausted, I found my way back to the ship. The snow white Rumanian steamer carried us through the swift waters of the Hellespont (the Dardanelles), past shadowy islands, out into the Ægean Sea, the purple sea of Ulysses.

The last night on the boat, I sat up in my deck chair. I felt awake to the eerie world around me—the starlit heaven and unknown sea. In the morning light as we neared the shore, I saw black goats in meadows of asphodel and ruins of gleaming white in dark olive groves. . . . This was ancient Greece. I had never dreamed it could still be so beautiful. The phantom voyage had returned to the earth; the illusion was ended. Sacred Mount Olympus ascended before us.

My three weeks' sojourn in Greece was a time of quiet happiness. My anxious eyes learned that the Parthenon was real. I longed to touch the broken stones, all that was left in marble by the master, Phidias, who had not only conceived the sacred temple of the Parthenon but had designed and supervised and with his own hands helped to create this majestic work in all its details. Fragments alone remained of the statuary, and some of the parts of the pediments and friezes; but of the glory that was the interior of the temple, the wonder of the ancient world, nothing at all remained.

The friezes had once been covered with subjects chosen from Attic mythology, riders and horses of the Panathenaic festival. The idea of those horses (long since removed to the British Museum) fascinated me the most, and I reread everything I could find about them. My family had English friends in Piræus. One Athenian, an archeologist, gave me access to his library, which contained more volumes than I could hope to investigate in my brief stay. Three weeks went by with the speed of a single day as I roamed the citadel of the Greek city and browsed through the books in the library of my friend.

He generously shared with me his speculations on the origin of the Parthenon type of the Thessalian horse (a cross with a Scythian breed): "In the most archaic types of the ninth and tenth centuries B.C.," he told me, "one could see the influence of Arabian blood; that is, anterior by five centuries to the time of highest development in Greek art. Unfortunately, no fossil remains of a native Greek horse have ever been found."

He settled many questions for me, questions that had worried me ever since as a child I had begun to look with the eyes of love upon the picture above my bed. He told me the Greeks rarely represented a horse in its natural gait. In most cases the artists had chosen the pace which pleased them.

The Athenian knight rarely rode his horse for pleasure but used him often in contests in the arena. Only in battle was the horse his equal and partner. The animal was honored, yet not loved. Some of the ancient bridle bits that I saw proved this last point. Though most of the horses have their mouths open, bits are seldom seen in statuary or on friezes. Large discs were placed upon the bits to keep the jaws apart. A cruel habit, but it suited the ancient artist.

So much that had never been clear to me was revealed now, through this friend—even facts about feeding, grooming, shoeing, and branding of horses in that classic period of Greece. The archeologist and I also pored over reproductions of Assyrian bas-reliefs with mounted lion-hunters. We almost dissected with our eyes a team of Egyptian horses, luminous as the sun, in Pharaoh's chariot at Karnak. With him I gazed intently at a colored picture of a Sassanide bowl showing spear-throwing warriors upon fleet desert horses, and we held in our hands under a magnifying glass a small decadrachma of Syracuse which showed a steed of the Libyan desert standing under a palm tree.

These creatures seemed paragons of perfection, of immortal beauty. These models must have lived, I thought, for the ancient masters were famous for the faithful likeness of their work to the original. . . .

But I received no answer to my question, where these horses and their offspring were to be found today. Then, quite by accident, I found in my friend's library a book called: *A Pilgrimage to Nejd*, by Lady Anne Blunt, written in 1881.

The next ten days I sat on the marble steps of the Parthenon in the shadow of the great columns and read—or rather translated page by page—this revealing book of Lady Anne Blunt. My Latin, French, and an English-German dictionary helped me to gather the meaning of the English, with which I was unfamiliar.

At the end of the tenth day I awoke from a dream. With great effort I had finished the first of the two volumes, which comprised Lady Anne Blunt's *Pilgrimage to Nejd*. I had traveled with her to Hayil, the Shammar capital in central Arabia. I had met her Bedouins, the nomadic tribes of the peninsula. In spirit, I had crossed the red sand desert too— that mysterious Nufud, the cradle of the Arabian horse.

And from the reading of this book there was let down into my consciousness a new world—spacious and free. The dignity and simplicity of an ancient life was there. I felt that in such an atmosphere and among such classic surroundings the ideal horse must also have been preserved uncontaminated— though Lady Anne Blunt gave no hint of it, nor was she describing animals resembling the Parthenon type. Even of the famous mares of Prince Ibn Rashid in Hayil, the author spoke as if they were only ordinary though very lovely creatures.

Perhaps Lady Anne Blunt's book had fired my youthful imagination too much, but I could not deny that my faltering hope had been strengthened. I had faith now—sufficient faith to believe that among the horses of the Bedouins some might be found as perfect and beautiful as the Athenian horses.

The mere word "Arabian" was enough to throw me back to those youthful memories still bright in my mind—the hollow cymbal ring of the King's dapple-grey Arabian, recalling the day when Prince Ernst rode his steed, then almost white, into the pool, and the intelligent horse had caught and played with his own image in the mirror of the water.

Tormented by all that I had not seen in Greece, I had to rejoin the party of teachers and students for my return to Dresden on the Balkan Express. A yearning for the distant desert had possessed my heart—a yearning as intense as the desire in my childish heart to see the world beyond the hills. This journey to Greece, the pilgrimage to the divine hill where my old heroes slept, was the beginning of my odyssey.

After my return from Athens I could no longer see my future in Europe. I still loved my books, and their heroes were still my friends, but they were as dead as ancient Greece was dead. I wanted to know living heroes in a living land. Within a few weeks I had turned my inner life upside down. I began to read about Arabia. I bought a grammar and tried to learn the intricate language.

In the midst of my new studies, out of the blue sky a letter came from a cousin, asking if I would like to assist his manager in Cairo. I leaped to this opportunity as a deer leaps from the open cage of his captors. My cousin did not know of my secret desire for Arabia. I had not dared to mention it. I was, I am sure, the most surprised member of my own family. I remained silent, crediting the astonishing event to the unknown power of desire: everything seems to be created first within us before it becomes an event—a reality.

My cousin's substantial offer, with a definite future assured, won the consent of my parents. Nothing prevented my sailing to Egypt. Now I was glad I had been taught to study seriously. The friends I had made in books, old and new, would not be a burden to me but an inspiration, a helping hand toward the goal for which I was blindly groping. The goal, I felt, would become my life.

About five in the morning I had my first view of Africa from the prow of the ship. We moved in that stillness that comes just before dawn, when all other noises of the ship are hushed, save the clank of its machinery and the rush of the water past the bow. I heard only the swirl of the bowsprit as it cut the smooth, oily surface of the water and tossed up a small ridge of white. The morning star glistened steadily, alone in the luminous green sky. Now and then a faraway lighthouse flashed its yellow beams over the sea.

As if drawn by a magnet, the boat drifted toward a shallow bank in the east. The first glow of dawn cast a rosy flush upon the water, revealing a small strip of coast—a ridge of solid gold that seemed to be built upon the sparkling sea, dotted with square little houses and lofty palm trees and graceful minarets beside a rounded dome.

The boat pulled up to the pier at Alexandria, ancient gateway to Egypt. Hundreds of gesticulating porters, guides, and vendors blocked my way, before I found myself in a landau, riding along a wide palm-lined boulevard. . . .

Ghazal—The Drinker of the Wind

THE NEXT DAY, speeding by train to Cairo, I was fascinated by the freight boats with their immense lateen sails, gliding like giant birds with glistening outspread wings along the Mahmudiyeh Canal. It was a strange sight, for one could rarely catch a glimpse of the canal itself. Its high banks served as connecting roads between the villages and were alive with natives and animals. The white sails swept silently past lush green fields, dark groves of date palms, brown mud-brick villages, minarets, and white domes of buried saints.

The date palms hung heavy with bundles of purple and yellow fruit. The land was rich and strange and beautiful, but the Bedouins were still a dream, and as yet I saw no fleet, proud steed.

Within my mind, however, I already possessed these deserts and Arabs and their horses. I refused to worry. I would renew my faith in their reality. I remembered my mother's words to me: "Be faithful and patient. . . ."

And I looked again upon the fleeting green countryside, heard the thin whistle of the train as it rushed toward Cairo. . . .

Al-Kahira, the victorious one—Cairo, the great metropolis of Africa, was a bewildering new city; its native atmosphere much more oriental than that of Alexandria, the city was to me a page from a fabulous story book.

It took me only a few days to realize that I had touched one of the most interesting cities in the world—vivid, too, by reason of the surrounding country: acres of ancient ruins, the ever-changing scenes of Egyptian farm life, and the desert which was still to me a tantalizing mystery. I longed to go beyond those hills.

However, as I roamed Cairo, I admitted to myself that I was not yet equipped to go to Arabia. I must study the language for at least another year before I would dare to venture forth into the desert.

After a few weeks in Egypt, I began to organize my days. I was quartered in the apartment of an Austrian family, as a result of letters of introduction which I had brought with me. My cousin's business was running smoothly: an office had been rented, a secretary hired, his imported goods arranged for display.

But I realized that this kind of life was not to my liking. I had never had business experience; I had been brought up with other ideals, and they were not those of an import concern.

Every morning, before going to the office, I crossed the Nile on the great Kasr-en-Nile bridge, and roamed the Island of Gezireh or watched the British officers at polo practice.

If only I could have a horse again, I thought. But how could I afford it? Save every penny to buy an old Egyptian nag, and then hobble through the parks? No, I would rather wait until I could have the kind of horse of which I had dreamed. Enviously, I watched the English and native grooms exercise their horses, some of which must have been almost pure-bred Arabians, though they were either country-bred (Egyptians) or importations from Syria.

At the end of four months I was suddenly informed that my cousin's firm had been sold to another concern in Europe and that my services were no longer required. A week later I was offered the position of an assistant manager of a plantation in lower Egypt, near Alexandria. I would have to work on the plantation under the supervision of an Egyptian manager, called Butrus, and his foreman, Ost'ahmed, to learn at first hand irrigation and Egyptian farming. I knew very little about agriculture beyond the knowledge I had acquired during four summer vacations on the experimental farm of relatives in Europe. But I could learn. . . .

I shall never forget my first impression on that faraway morning when Butrus, the manager, introduced me to my new surroundings.

The day was warm, the air dry and scented with myrtle; the blue sky melted into the azure of the sea beyond; turtle-doves cooed in lofty branches of stately trees; from among hibiscus bushes, aflame with blossoms, peered a gazelle with shining dark eyes. Gracefully the tame animal walked across the gravel walk to a murmuring fountain and quenched its thirst. From a building in Moorish Kiosk-style—which was the stables—a servant led toward me a young Arabian stallion.

My heart filled with wonder and joy at the sight. I hoped that among the horses of this stud I might find a perfect type, but my heart sank when one after the other the horses were brought out to be inspected and I could not find a single one of my ideal creatures, which in the frieze of the Parthenon achieve perfection.

27

The horses he showed to me could not deceive a seeker after the authentic blood. Their plain heads lacked entirely the characteristics of the picture in my mind. They had ordinary features with small eyes and most of them were high-legged. However, when they were in an excited state, prancing about, they showed the charm and grace of the Arabian type. They had tails of fine hair, carried high, and an iridescent sheen on their satin coats.

Butrus, the plantation manager, called them country-bred (Egyptians) and Syrians.

"Not Arabians?" I asked.

"Not imported from the desert," Butrus answered, "but from the villages."

I felt immensely relieved that these animals were not authentic Arabians. I thought of my quest and the final goal in my heart; the desert and the tribes among whom I could still hope to find the high-caste Arabian. On the spur of the moment I revealed my ideal to Butrus and suggested to him that an importation of brood mares and some stallions from the desert might help him to produce a much better type.

Butrus admitted that such an importation would not only be an unusual opportunity to improve his stud, but also to make a good deal of money on the side. He suggested that I stay at least a year on the plantation to better acquaint myself with the mind and language of Arabs and learn more about their horses and the breeding from a practical standpoint. Then I could look for some Bedouin or other native from Arabia and make the journey into the desert with him.

I visualized already the fulfillment of my most cherished hopes—to discover on such an expedition into the Arabian desert the lost horse of antiquity.

I had not been long on the plantation when my sixteen-year-old sister, Charlotte, joined me. She was soon as important a part of the household—and of my idea of Egypt—as if she had always lived in the villa and had always looked out for its wide-spreading acacias and its flaming bougain-villea. . . .

One morning we rode to the plantation together. We left in the quiet hour just before dawn, when our garden was still sweet with the fragrance of night. We rode past the sea-shore, through the awakening palm grove, haunted by the deep plaints of mourning doves.

In the evening we returned with Butrus, the manager of the plantation. We wound our way past the Mahmudiyeh Canal, glistening in the starlight, full of subdued sound as white sails rustled on their great, squeaking masts. Small eve-ning fires burned on deck, and the water swished softly past the bow of the boats. We passed an age-old mound which became alive with dark shapes. Howls and cries pursued us and a pack of dogs shot across the road, snarling and snapping at our horses.

We galloped for safety toward the nearby village with these curs at our heels. In safety we reached the settlement, to be told that cattle had been dying. The carcasses had been thrown upon the mound, and from far and wide dogs were coming to feast.

We decided to take another route home, along the brackish swamps of the lake. A heavy mist rose from the water. Na-tives on their camels and water buffaloes formed eerie shapes in the strange light.

Through clover and vegetable fields we trotted briskly until we reached a few whitewashed houses in a palm grove. Beyond the tree trunks flickering lights marked a group of black tents at the foot of a sand dune. Here a wealthy desert chief lived in a modern villa, built like a stronghold. Some of his retainers, people of the desert, had settled next to him.

"Sons of jackals!" Butrus muttered. "Robbers! Killers!"

Like all the Levantines and fellahin (peasants), he despised and feared the Arabs of the desert, but nevertheless, I asked Charlotte to ride up to one of the tents with me. Though warned by our companion, we pressed our horses forward.

In the tent nearest us, three robed men rose and came out to greet us. Ancient lances were stuck in the sand near the women's part of the tent. Charlotte and I dismounted at the threshold.

"May your night be of good omen," I greeted them like a Franki (European).

"And may your night be happy," they answered. "Come in. Why do you stand outside?"

Observing that a girl was with me, they called the Hurma, the chief woman. She was of middle age and unveiled. Graciously she led Charlotte to her section of the tent.

As I followed the three Bedouins, I heard laughter from next door, and knew that Charlotte, unable to understand the women and children, must be amusing to them.

I explained to the men that she was my sister and had arrived only recently from Europe, that this was the first time she had entered a Bedouin tent. Our host, professing to be deeply honored, joined his wife and children to tell them the important news. Luckily I overheard his order to have a young goat killed in our honor.

"Not tonight!" I cried.

It was difficult to dissuade him from sacrificing the goat, until we had promised to return another day to partake of the meat in the Bedouin's abode. Moreover, we were not al-

lowed to leave until we had tasted coffee and a morsel of
bread—tokens of friendship.

"Accept the comforts from Allah," our host said. Later he
told us that they were journeying to Montazah, toward the
Well of the Dreamer, to camp with other Arabs on the field
of Sidi Ohn, to take part in a native festival, where, by the
end of the week, all the best riders of Egypt would meet.

"Thy horse will lift ye to ride on the wind," the man flat-
tered me, pointing to my horse, Filfil. I denied that Filfil was
fast enough to compete in an open race. But the persuasive
powers of my host were such that I promised to visit with
Charlotte the rider-festival at Montazah.

We mounted again and rode home with the blessings of
our host upon us. "And you call them scoundrels?" I asked
Butrus. "Jackals and robbers? Shame on you!"

Charlotte looked back at the country of the fellah and the
Bedouin. "Don't they make you feel small, these children of
the desert!" she said.

"You feel that, too?" I asked.

All my dreams came back to me, more real and more com-
pelling than ever, and I said to Charlotte, "Some day I must
know these people of the desert. I must find the beautiful
ancestral horse of the frieze on the Parthenon. But my quest
may be for a mythical horse which no longer exists."

2

THE MULID OF Sidi Ohn, the native festival to celebrate the birth of an Egyptian saint, turned out to be the occasion for a great gathering of fellahin and semi-nomad Arabs of Lower Egypt.

Upon a wide plain bordered by sand dunes and date groves, long rows of tents had been set up. Freaks, jugglers, snake-charmers, musicians, and sword-swallowers thronged the carnival.

Acrobats and wire-walkers operated in the midst of the crowd, as did the pickpockets, who, when caught, were flogged by the bystanders and released to resume their hazardous profession. An Ulema, aided by a Koran-reader, struggled vainly to reach the ears of those who were lost to the sinful attraction of the glass-eater and a card-shark.

Charlotte and I handed our horses to some attendants out in the open beyond the tents, as most of the visiting riders had done. But Butrus, riding his beautiful white donkey, insisted on leaving his animal under a shelter. He did not want to take a chance that his "Eye's Delight" might be injured or stolen.

Butrus and his donkey were a sight. Our friend wore an antique Turkish costume and had added to his immense sash a silver dagger and two exquisite Persian pistols. They must have been relics of the sixteenth or seventeenth century, richly inlaid with silver and with muzzles as big as post horns. To enhance the glory of his donkey, Butrus had rubbed red henna into the white tail and mane. The animal looked very "dashing" with this new note of color and the gay ornaments of bridle and saddle. To his relief Butrus discovered an old acquaintance, a snake-charmer who had set up a reed hut, which was just the kind of quarters Butrus desired to have for his mount. The snake-charmer's gypsy wife promised to keep an eye on Butrus' painted donkey.

I made arrangements to ride Filfil in the Sidi Ohn race, for I was curious to know how speedy and surefooted he could be. The competing horses must run the length of the field twice—a three-mile race. The last stretch was an uphill run, ending in front of the official committee's tents, where two flags marked the finish. The race was scheduled for late in the afternoon. Seventy horses were to take part. Only these tough little country-bred horses could have stood the rough ground, the dangerous melee of riders and animals, and an Egyptian summer day. I used my English polo saddle with stirrups. Others in the race were seated on high-pommeled African saddles, on Syrian and Egyptian riding pads, or were mounted bareback. Neither the weight of riders and equipment nor the condition, weight, or age of the horses counted. Most of the competitors hailed from the provinces, though many semi-Bedouins could be found among them. These half-nomadic Arabs came from the Gharbiyeh and Dak-Haliyeh districts, the western desert of Egypt and the Fayum. Fair-skinned and bronzed Arabs mingled with Negroes and some white men from Alexandria.

A venerable village chief from the neighborhood of Rosetta sat as judge of the race upon a dais in his tent, surrounded by notables and servants. Each competitor rode up to the pavilion, dismounted, walked with his horse to the dais, and kissed the old man's hand. He usually had a word or two for the rider, sometimes he asked that the horse be led close enough for him to touch its forehead and say: "Masha'llah."

When Filfil followed me up to the stand without any guidance, the old gentleman clapped his hands in surprise. I kissed the tips of his fingers and wished him long life and peace. Observing that I was a foreigner and unbeliever, he sat up very straight and looked seriously at me.

"Italiani?" he asked.

I smiled and threw up my chin and clucked my tongue, which in Arabic corresponds to our shaking the head in denial.

"Be on thy way, my son," the patriarch said in friendly manner. "My eyes will follow thee."

On a nearby hill a mortar was discharged. The shot was a signal for the riders to assemble for the race. Seventy shouting, cheering men tried to collect and calm their prancing, squealing steeds. One of the men pointed out to me an Egyptian rider in the uniform of the Khedive's bodyguard. "This man is called Al-'Attab—the intrepid horseman—and the date-colored stallion he rides is the gift of Faisal ibn Rashid of Hayil to the Khedive of Egypt," he informed me.

The stallion was a racy type, perhaps three inches taller than Filfil, and proportionately larger. He had a long straight profile with small eyes, lacking Arabian characteristics, and neck and legs longer than those of the Egyptian horses I knew.

"He is a Mu'niqui Hadraji," the man explained, "the fastest strain of the desert horse."

"He looks like an English thoroughbred," I said. I knew

that the man would understand my comparison, for the Egyptians see many English race horses on the tracks in Alexandria.

"Yes," was his reply. "This horse may have the speed, but he lacks the endurance to win a very long race."

"Then my horse should not be afraid of the Khedive's stallion," I said.

"No, don't fear to stay behind at the beginning of the race," the man tipped me off.

I looked around. The crowd was watching a soldier light a match to the fuse of a second mortar. Our horses plunged and snorted, while the frenzied crowd screamed at the top of their lungs. With a thundering crash the bomb exploded— we were off.

Filfil was swept along in a wave of riders and horses, but he pressed forward through the thick of the line and raced toward the opposite side of the field. The Khedive's thoroughbred was well in the lead; he reached the line at the end of the field, turned about, and tore back into us. Filfil and other horses swerved aside and rushed across the line, whirling around to follow the leader. Horses and riders dashed into each other. Some were thrown headlong upon the field. Many horses stampeded blindly against the solid wall of spectators, then hurled themselves back into the race, the deafening cheers of the crowd following them.

Filfil was behind the first twenty horses. But after awhile he raced along among the first ten, with the Khedive's horse still in the lead. On the last stretch, ending in front of the pavilion and the dais of the old judge, Filfil overtook the Khedivial rider and finished neck and neck with two other horses to be awarded fourth place. But the winner, a Bedouin riding six lengths ahead of all the horses, stopped his mare at the judge's stand. The little animal turned on her heels, reared straight into the air, while the man on her back fired his rifle. Then the mare spun around, wildly galloped away into the desert, and disappeared. Nobody knew who horse and rider were or where they had come from.

"Kilab—wild dogs of the desert," Butrus said when I asked him.

I was proud of Filfil and amazed that he had made such a fine showing. The winners were lined up on a ceremonial carpet before the dais. The old judge laid his right palm upon each horse in blessing and presented the prizes to the riders: a silver watch as second prize to the man upon the Barb stallion, a turquoise ring for the third rider, an ornamental woolen halter for Filfil, and a pair of hobbles for the fifth horse.

The winners were asked to ride behind the musicians as they led the procession down hill through the race course. Behind us followed the manager of the Khedivial stable in Montazah and a troop of police and notables. In an open landau with a driver and a servant holding a parasol over him, rode the white-bearded judge.

At the opposite end of the grounds the procession came to a halt. The cheering crowd had increased to a great number, overflowing into the dunes. Long shadows were cast across the field, and the air was cool for the first time that day.

Riding events followed one after another until dusk fell upon the jubilant crowd. The music continued, and storytellers wove through the throng. The Arab cemetery was a field of bobbing red and green lanterns and the moving shadows of women and children.

At last Charlotte and I mounted our horses to join Butrus. Who could describe the fury and despair in which we found him? When he returned to claim his dazzling mount, he found that the good gypsy wife of the snake-charmer had neglected her duty as guardian, going off to mingle with the gossiping women in the cemetery. The animal's henna-stained mane and tail were gone. Someone had played a trick on Butrus and shorn the donkey of its glory. Henna hair lay about the floor of the hut in strands of various lengths.

But Butrus was quickly enlightened and the real culprit uncovered. The snake-charmer's mule had chewed off the donkey's mane and tail. Now again, as we stood by the mule, he began to chew the stubbles that were left of the mane and the tail of the donkey. To all appearances Butrus' "Eye's Delight" liked it. It tickled him, and he twitched his nose and curled his lips as he relished the chafing and rasping of the mule's yellow teeth.

Butrus' rage was complete. He pulled both of the prehistoric pistols from his sash to shoot the mule, but an angry crowd howled in protest. Then Butrus also remembered that the guns had not been loaded since Napoleon fought at the Pyramids. With a flourish he returned them to his sash. He looked in vain for another and more dignified mount to take him back to the plantation, but he had to ride his donkey after all.

3

MY DAYS became a routine of work on the plantation
and week ends with Charlotte and our friends at Ramleh
beach. It was a year and a half now since I had left Europe;
more than a year I had allowed myself to sacrifice in order
to study Arabic and become acquainted with the people of
the Near East. Then the unseen hand on the steering wheel
of life guided me out upon a new and, as it seemed, uncharted
sea.

One morning Filfil and I were trotting beside an irrigation
canal near Sidi Bishr. The shadow of night had vanished.
Through the grey dawn glimmered the faint light of the
awakening day. On the eastern horizon showed the dark
silhouettes, solemn and square, of an Egyptian village. We
took a short-cut along the Rosetta railroad, turned west, and
were soon hidden in tall rushes, beyond which stretched
miles of fresh green plants—cotton, the white gold of Egypt.
The scent of the fruitful earth rose to my nostrils.

The world was well awake.

Riders loomed ahead of us. As they drew closer, I noticed
that one, trotting briskly on a grey donkey, was a fellah.
The other was a white-bearded Bedouin, mounted on a small
horse. The poor animal looked very rough and abused, as if
it had just been brought in from a very long journey in the

desert. But there was something about this emaciated little chestnut stallion that fascinated me, though he was not much to look at and certainly had not been groomed for ages past. He had four white feet, and a white star on his forehead—a head bold and angular as jagged rock. And his enormous eyes were like those of a gazelle.

Even after the men had passed from sight, I retained a mental picture of the brave little animal, recalling his balanced motions and the soft champ of his teeth.

"Thou shalt not covet thy neighbor's horse," I warned myself, and touched Filfil to carry me on, but I soon halted him to look back once more. Not a soul could be seen. Only the tall bamboo reeds rustled lightly. I confess I had fallen in love with that creature, rough and small though he appeared, and far from the picture I envisioned the Bedouin horse to be.

For some reason I could not rid myself of the memory of the Bedouin's horse. As I held him before my inner eyes, I was afraid—afraid that I would never see him nor his like again.

On an impulse, I wheeled Filfil around and galloped back. He took the reins and raced like a thoroughbred, thinking perhaps that we were returning to the stable. Beyond the first curve of the road I caught sight of the two riders. I changed Filfil to a slower gait, and we trotted closer to the pair. The Bedouin's horse became excited as we approached. His bright eyes glanced sideways to bring me into his range of vision; his little ears twitched to and fro. He snorted furiously and pawed the ground, but with a few firm strokes of his master's hand he became quiet.

"As-salam alayk—peace be with you," the Bedouin called out to me in a most friendly fashion.

I was accustomed to being ignored by the Arabs when I wore European garb—a tropical helmet and khaki riding breeches. But this man greeted me jovially and asked questions in a quick and curious, but pleasant, way and the Egyptian peasant listened mutely to our conversation as we rode on.

The rider on the stallion was Sheykh Ammer ibn-al-Aide. He belonged to the Wuld Ali, a migrating tribe of Arabia, and had come to Egypt to visit his relatives in the Libyan desert.

Our little group rode past the barns of a big domain. Cattle were being fed, and all manner of animal sounds reached our ears. A pump creaked and splashed its muddy water into long troughs, and a turkey tried to waylay us, wings scraping the ground.

Here at the edge of the sown land the fellah left us, and the Bedouin invited me to ride with him to his camp in the desert. Only a solitary date palm and some tamarisk bushes marked the spot where a black goathair tent rose from the ground. Slaves came out to receive us, while the sheykh, with the agility of a young man, dismounted.

"You haven't told me your horse's name," I said.

The old man smiled and for answer clapped his hands sharply. In an instant the stallion whirled about and galloped away from us. He had taken hardly more than a dozen strides when the sheykh called out, "Irja Ghazal—back to me, Ghazal."

Gazelle! A fitting name.

"My daughter was the first to call him the gazelle," the old man explained with pride. "He is indeed a *Drinker of the Wind*."

As we sat down in Sheykh Ammer's tent, the old chief

40

poured coffee into a tiny cup from one of the beaked cans that stood in the glowing embers. "Welcome to the threshold of our sanctuary," he said with exquisite formality.

In the wilderness every home is a retreat where the stranger's stay may lengthen into years, where his past is his own. Abraham entertained angels unaware. Since that day the Bedouin says, "We look upon the visiting stranger as an envoy of our Lord."

I settled down beside his fireplace with my new friend. It was comfortable in the nomad booth, not close or stagnant as in a white canvas tent. The coarsely woven black goathair allowed the air to circulate freely through the curtains.

A slave placed a camel saddle at my left for me to lean upon. I found that position close to the ground very comfortable. The horizon came almost to a level with my eyes, and the interior of the tent could also be seen from an unusual angle. Such differences in the mode of life were not only novel, but they also carried me closer to the natural perspective of Arabian existence. Spiritually, perhaps, they were symbolic of the humble and close-to-the-earth attitude of the desert man and of that ancient life which—I had feared—might no longer exist. Now I was conscious of my identity with this new world in which I hoped to discover paragons of beauty and perfection in horses. In Ghazal, the rough emaciated little desert stallion, I had not found the realization of my dreams, but he established for me a contact which I had eagerly looked for. He showed many points of conformation to Arabian characteristics which might be found in greater quality in animals of his breeding among the tribes. I admitted to myself that my quest was perhaps only kindled by a romantic impulse in my young soul, that possibly the horse of perfection might no longer exist. But

I consoled myself that I had found at last one authentic horse of the desert, which might lead me to the finest of its kind among the Bedouins of Arabia.

Urged on by my interest in his stallion, the sheykh offered to show me an example of Ghazal's intelligence. The horse had not only been taught the meaning of thirty-seven words, but he understood also the purpose of many gestures of his master's hand.

As he walked away from the tent, the sheykh suddenly threw himself full length upon the ground. Ghazal, some distance away, snorted in fright and at once wheeled about, racing at full speed to the side of his master. He pawed the ground beside him and neighed loudly. When the sheykh did not respond, Ghazal tried to turn his master's body over with his nose and nipped at him with anxious little caresses.

"Ghazal!" whispered the sheykh.

At once the horse sought the ground, his muzzle close to the man's face.

"Naum—sleep!" the sheykh said, and with a deep sigh Ghazal went down on his forelegs, bent his hocks and settled upon the sand, rolling over on his side.

Now the sheykh crawled across Ghazal's withers and seated himself upon his back.

"Goom—arise!" he called out.

With no apparent strain Ghazal lifted his body to a kneeling position, then rose from his haunches to stand firmly on his feet.

Rewarding Ghazal with a friendly slap on the croup, the sheykh commanded, "Zatt—throw."

Instantly Ghazal rose on his hindfeet, pawing the air, his whole body aquiver. Though Sheykh Ammer's hands were buried firmly in Ghazal's mane, he lost his hold and slipped from the back of the horse and on to his feet.

Absent-mindedly I touched the shoulder of Sheykh Ammer to congratulate him. "Beware!" cried the sheykh. But before I was aware what his shout meant, I was bowled over by Ghazal, who had rushed between us. While I brushed the dust from my back, the old man scolded Ghazal and sent him away with a single gesture, saying, "Enough of these tricks." Turning to me, the sheykh said, "I did not expect Ghazal to treat you so roughly. He ought to have known that you are a friend, not a foe."

We returned to our camel-saddle seats near the coffee hearth. A strong aroma of crushed coffee beans and the scented smoke of tamarisk wood filled the air. Savory odor drifted to us from another quarter, in which a servant busily handled the meat pots of the little nomad household.

Just before the meal was served, Sheykh Ammer left the tent to pray. Silently and solemnly he knelt, with his slave a short distance away. They placed the palms of their hands against their cheeks, thumbs touching the ears, and called out the Takbir ("God is the most high") and repeated the prayers of the so-called four Rek'ahs. After a while the slave rose, but the sheykh held his hands before him like an open book upon which he fixed his gaze. As he passed his hands from his brow to his face, he began the salutations of the last prayer. I thought he must be imploring God for a special favor, for I caught anxiety in his voice.

The prayer ended, Sheykh Ammer again seated himself at my side. His young daughter, Adla, came running in, and he embraced her. Nestling in her father's arms, she watched me curiously.

"Let us break our fast," said my host.

The slaves spread a rug at our feet and on the rug a leather cover, and upon that a large platter with rice and roasted pigeons stuffed with tamarinds and small onions.

We ate without knife or fork. The trick was to squeeze a handful of rice into an egg-shaped ball or tear a morsel of the thin, pancake-like bread for a scoop in carrying rice and meat to the mouth. Now and then the old sheykh selected a choice piece of meat from the pile before us and handed this delicacy to me. For dessert we had small honey cakes, cooked in almond milk with nuts and dates; also juicy melons and tangerines. This was not the wild fare of inner Arabia but the offering of the sown land of Egypt.

During the meal a rider, mounted on a small fawn-colored race camel, trotted up to our tent.

"Marzuki," the sheykh cried in welcome.

The newcomer, I learned, had once been the royal stable master of the Khedive of Egypt. Born in Buryada, in central Arabia, some forty years before, Marzuki had spent a good share of his life in Cairo and Stambul. He was often sent on special missions to purchase horses from desert chiefs of inner Arabia for the Sultan of Turkey and the pashas in Egypt.

Marzuki was slender and apparently frail, but he had a reputation for great prowess. I marveled at the smallness of his hands and feet. His lean, weather-beaten face was gentle in spite of the aquiline nose, alert dark eyes, and heavy brows. Across his left cheek flared a livid scar which, strangely enough, did not disfigure him. That and his pointed black beard made him an oddly distinguished figure, one of natural grace and dignity.

I soon found out that Marzuki was a poet, skilled in writing odes in the manner of the ancient Arabs. He sang poems to the accompaniment of a lute, the rhubaba. A desert troubadour was Marzuki—and like all of his kind, a fellow with an unfailing sense of humor.

He had packed away in his saddlebag a large manuscript of parchment leaves covered with several hundred poems he had written. In our presence he began to compose, offhand, a song about the hero of heroes—Marzuki himself. The sheykh shook a finger at him. "Marzuki," he said, "nothing short of death will stop thy flow of poetry."

When he heard of my interest in Arabian horses and that I might go to Damascus to purchase some animals, Marzuki took on a serious mien. He offered to leave with me for Syria any time that I was ready to go. He visited Arabia every year, he said, to trade in camels and horses among the tribes. "I shall find for you a dhalul—a race camel," he promised, "a fleet one of great endurance, and I will be your guide to the Arabs in the Hamad and Nufud deserts."

I thanked Marzuki for his trust in me, a total stranger, and a man not of his faith.

"But we are of one brotherhood," he assured me, "because you love the Arabs, and they are my people."

I could not help reflecting upon the adventure that had so unexpectedly befallen me these last few hours. Beyond that sudden vision of the desert horse, this new world was opening to me—a world of which I, man of the west, as yet had little comprehension. Now I was removed almost by ages from the civilization with which I had been familiar in Europe. And men I had met only a few hours before were to become lifelong friends.

Sheykh Ammer called us and walked with us some distance away from the tent. Extending both hands, he signaled to

Ghazal. At once the stallion galloped to us. The halter had slipped from his head, and he stood before us as God had created him. There were not even shoes on his feet.

I sensed at that moment that, as completely and harmoniously as this palm tree belonged to the sand dune, so in the phenomena of the spaceless, timeless picture, Ghazal and Sheykh Ammer had been drawn together forever in my mind.

Sheykh Ammer broke in upon my thoughts. "This is your opportunity to become acquainted with Ghazal." He picked up the headstall, slipped it over Ghazal's forehead, and laid a riding pad, made from a cheetah skin, upon his back, and fastened the girth.

Taking my right hand in his own, the sheykh extended it to the stallion's nostrils. For a split-second Ghazal's ears went back. It was as if a spark of distrust that had lived in him toward me had suddenly flicked away. Cautiously his soft nose touched my hand. His lips fumbled searchingly from my palm to my finger tips. He wanted to know me more intimately by my scent. Inhaling and exhaling cautiously, his warm breath flowed over my skin. Then I felt the touch of his muzzle upon my cheeks and eyes and ears. In playful mood Ghazal wheeled about me, snorting and sniffling as though trying to discover if I were only an apparition to be blown away.

But I talked to him and lifted my hand to his nostrils and allowed him to rub his forehead against me. He laid his head upon my shoulder. Trustingly, instinctively, he had decided the question of our friendship.

Sheykh Ammer smiled his pleasure that Ghazal had chosen me. "I have parted with him. I have decided to lend my horse

46

to you," he said. "You may ride Ghazal on your journey to Damascus with our friend Marzuki."

"But I cannot accept the loan of Ghazal!" I cried.

"With your consent, it is arranged. Marzuki and I have talked it over. And when you have finished your visit to the tribes, you may return Ghazal to me."

I offered to arrange some kind of payment for the use of his horse, but he became angry and said to me, "Ghazal is like unto one of our children. We cannot sell our horses for gold, but we entrust them to our friends."

I looked again at the creature of the uncloven hoofs whom he called Ghazal, the black-skinned antelope of the desert, the Drinker of the Wind.

"I am honored," the sheykh said, "that you ride my stallion to Arabia. Compare him to others you will see in the desert."

I was not allowed to say another word of refusal, and Marzuki came and smiled, saying, "I was fearful, lest Ghazal might not love thee. . . ."

"I begged Sheykh Ammer not to part with him," I explained to Marzuki.

"But our friend is not losing Ghazal," Marzuki assured me. "I promised to look after the horse and you and to bring you both safely back from Damascus."

Marzuki then looked at my riding breeches and tropical sun helmet. They would not do, he said, if I were to ride the horse of the desert. He ordered a slave to bring a bundle of Bedouin clothing from the depths of a camel saddlebag.

It was exciting to exchange my breeches and polo shirt for long-sleeved robes and a white veil, the ends of which I was to tuck under the twisted black cord on the crown of my head. The slave helped me to pull off my riding boots. In their stead I wore a pair of soft gazelle-leather sandals. Then he placed a black shepherd coat upon my shoulders. It was so comfortable that I would have been ready to promise never to wear anything else.

When I stepped up to Ghazal and put my hand in his mane and mounted him, he sensed the friend under the familiar garb, and whinnied softly.

"Bismillah—in the name of God!" the sheykh cried.

Animated by his master's words, Ghazal settled back on his haunches. For a moment he pawed the air; then he plunged forward with a few bold leaps. He was in playful mood, but when I called out his name and pressed my legs lightly to his ribs, he collected himself. And when I offered a more severe pressure behind his girth, and leaned forward, Ghazal fell into a canter.

Now he flew along at a full gallop. The song of winged hoofs had become true, the thrumming of the dainty feet of my gallant little gazelle—the swallower of the ground. . . .

His powerful neck rose before me, "strong as a tower of refuge," Job of old had said. "He rejoiceth in his strength, he mocketh at fear . . . when above him the spear and shield shall glitter . . . when the noise of the trumpet soundeth . . . the thunder of the captains and their shouting."

The soil beneath us was hard clay with a thin top layer of sand, ideal ground for a gallop. But I had no time to test Ghazal's endurance, nor even his real speed. With his small ears pricked back, he listened to my caressing words. With senses alert, he carried his head high on a crescent neck.

"Indak—halt!" I called the word by which I could prepare him to slow down from a flying gallop to a canter, then to a standstill. By a light touch on either side of his neck he could be brought to a still slower gait, and finally to a walk, and full stop.

I slipped from his back and talked to him, and he answered me with a soft cry. His high-arched tail rippled in the strong breeze. He stood motionless except for his panting flanks and extended nostrils, breathing quickly and snorting a few times with impatience.

When I walked off, Ghazal followed me. The wind soon dried his hair, and I smoothed it with my hands and mounted him again.

"Khatwa," I said, and with a strong and extended stride he walked away. On this homeward stretch he was gay-spirited. Our companionship filled me with joy, and the desert solitude and peace of approaching night stole into my heart.

The evening was deep with shadow when we neared Sheykh Ammer's tent. Ghazal neighed loudly at the sight of the other horses standing near a large herd of camels which had been brought in from pasture.

A light beeze fanned the folds of my shepherd coat and the scarf on my head as I rode toward the fire smoldering in Sheykh Ammer's tent. Like an island in the ocean of growing night was this lone palm oasis with its solitary great tent and its cluster of resting animals. A slave stirred the fire on the coffee hearth. The flames leaped high, lighting the dark nomad booth.

Adla, the little girl, appeared with a large wooden bowl of fresh camel's milk. Ghazal whinnied as the child came toward him with the foaming beverage. Down went his black muzzle into the white froth, and in one draught he emptied the vessel. Then, with foam-covered nose, he went over Adla's cheeks. Laughingly she accepted his caresses, return-

49

ing his affection with a kiss of her own on that soft spot above the side of his mouth.

Toward midnight Marzuki and I made preparations to leave Sheykh Ammer's family. All the members of the household came to say farewell. Bedouins rarely take sentimental leave of friends or even relatives. Setting forth on a long journey, they ride away without turning back or saying a word. But this time Sheykh Ammer made a ceremony of our parting. He brought forth a piece of parchment with these words of the Koran written upon it: "Blessed is the path of those to whom thou hast been gracious."

This parchment the old man folded and inserted in a silver hijab (amulet) which he attached by two little silver chains to Ghazal's headstall. Then he laid his hand in blessing upon Ghazal and wished the grace of God to all of us.

Some hours later our little cavalcade reached the outskirts of Ramleh. Ahead of me rode Marzuki on his camel, leading the much-neglected Filfil, past garden walls and hedges of cactus and fig shrubbery. The air was sweet with acacia and jasmine. Thick veils of bougainvillea covered the verandas of small villas set deep in their luxuriant gardens.

Ramleh, built on layers of rich, golden sand, is irrigated by Nile river water and caressed by the damp, warm air of the ocean. No wonder, then, that even in winter everything grows in profusion and that the rulers of the land have chosen for ages past to build their marble palaces on this stretch of coast, so favored by nature.

We urged our animals on into the night, discussing the inconsistencies of human nature. Fireflies darted brightly across our path.

"Blessed are those who are carriers of light," mused Marzuki.

50

He liked to exhibit his philosophical talents as well as his flair for poetry. But it was as a man of the desert, a brave companion, that I was to admire him most.

When we reached the smooth, cool sand of the beach, Ghazal walked courageously into the breakers. White foam swirled around his knees and splashed his chest. He loved the sea. In the pale light of the stars it looked as if legions of white horses rose from the ocean, endlessly and rhythmically to attack the shore with thundering hoofs. Forever they come in wild haste, and the wind followed them like their own breath, panting and shaking their white manes.

Marzuki dismounted to start a brisk fire of driftwood upon the beach. The colors of a false dawn shone palely and died away. We could not name them or catch them again.

I rode Ghazal to a rocky shelter under the palisades. Like eye sockets in a great skull, black caverns gazed blindly out over the ocean. Ancient tombs fashioned by the Greek rulers of old Egypt, they were empty now. The bodies once held in their stone embrace had been robbed of jewels and the bones left to the sea.

In one of these caves I took off my garments and placed them above the reach of the waves. Then I rode Ghazal into the tide again. He breasted the surf to reach the calm waters beyond. We drifted parallel to the shore, carried swiftly toward a long stretch of sandy beach, where my stallion rose out of the waves and shook the water from his shining coat. This feat Ghazal repeated several times, until Marzuki called us. Quickly I put on my clothes and seated myself near the fire.

4

BACK AT MY home in Ramleh, Marzuki was full of kind attention. He helped me to prepare for the journey to Damascus and settled satisfactorily the business end of the undertaking with Butrus, the manager of our plantation, who realized that I was of more value to him purchasing horses in Arabia than doing routine work on the plantation. Marzuki presented me with a pair of saddlebags for Ghazal. They were old Persian rugs, joined to form large pockets, handy for tucking away odds and ends, necessary for a long journey. Emptied, they covered Ghazal by night.

And from Marzuki I also learned how to shoe Ghazal in the fashion of desert people. The Arabian horseshoe, or na'l —the sandal—is a thin steel plate covering the entire surface of the hoof and having a small hole in the center. It is put on cold, after the plate has been bent to the desired shape in a charcoal or camel-dung fire.

Only three feet are shod. One hind hoof remains unshod to give a firm purchase on slippery ground or rocks. According to Marzuki, the "horse of the night" had lost one plate in its course through the sky. That solitary shoe which remained behind is, said he, our moon.

Before our departure Marzuki asked me to ride with him to fetch the race camel which he had promised me. On this little excursion we visited Sheykh Ammer's camp once more, but he had left to migrate with relatives in the Libyan desert.

On our way to Amrieh a railroad train came hissing and puffing along the shining tracks. Ghazal did not like the looks or speed of this clanking iron horse. At once he tried to out-distance his rival, while enthusiastic passengers leaned from the windows to encourage him with loud yells. The engineer joined in the fun.

Putting on a lot of steam, and with smoke billowing from the engine, he challenged Ghazal with the whistle's devilish screams. Ghazal's eyes bulged with excitement. He snorted defiance, and his little hoofs drummed away as if our very lives depended on his speed.

I knew Ghazal could not keep this up very long, and to spare him an inglorious end, I wheeled him about while he was still in the lead and bouncing along in his last heroic effort to outstrip the menacing creature. I turned him away to a nearby hill around which the train must make a detour.

Ghazal panted heavily as he scampered up the hill. He champed his teeth, and danced around when, from the brow of the incline, he looked down upon that belching monster, that fire-spitting reptile, which wriggled on its dark belly with unbelievable speed across the barren waste.

"I could trample him under my hoofs," Ghazal's manner seemed to say.

I stroked his mane and patted his neck and told him what a wonderful fellow he was. Perhaps I even made him feel that we owed our lives to his speed, for, indeed, Ghazal seemed taller by a few inches and prouder in bearing when we re-joined Marzuki, who trotted nonchalantly along on his camel.

Amrieh was a beautiful oasis at the foot of low hills near the sea. Here we were guests of an acquaintance of Marzuki, who occupied a house adjoining the village mosque and provided us with a room. He also allowed us the use of a paddock in his backyard for Ghazal.

Before going upstairs to my room, I took one more look at Ghazal and found him enjoying his feed. He came toward me and neighed, passing his lips over my face—his own way of wishing me good-night. . . .

Before dawn I awoke to the melodious chant of the Muezzin. Making the round on the high balcony of the minaret, he called to the four winds: "God alone is great. I testify there is no god but God! I confess that Mohammed is His Prophet! Come to prayer! Prayer is better than sleep!"

Life stirred as the morning call to prayer drifted over Amrieh. Lights appeared in many windows. At the edge of the desert men arose from coffee fires in Bedouin tents. Prayers rugs were spread out. Men turned their faces toward the east, to Mecca, where the first brightness of day appeared like a dim, distant silver breach in the night.

"Allah Akbar! Ahadu Anla, Laha Illa'llah . . ."

Down below me, in a narrow lane, a dark bundle also came to life—a blind beggar who had spent the night there rolled up in rags. He spread his tattered covers before him like a precious prayer rug and, standing upon them, he called out the Takbir and the Fathah: "Exalt thy God, O my soul! Exalt the perfection of my Lord the most high!" With hands outspread upon his thighs he dropped to his knees and inclined his head, first to the right and then to the left, in greeting to the unseen guardians of his soul.

Before joining Marzuki at the Greek café, I walked over to the paddock to greet Ghazal, but the enclosure was empty! The crossbar of the gate had been lifted, and the bolt hung neatly by its leather thong. Someone familiar with the place must have opened the gate and taken Ghazal away.

I called Marzuki and walked over with him to the enclosure to examine the evidence. There we found remains of munched hay and marks of Ghazal's teeth on the wooden bolt; also hairs from his mane, clinging to the rough edge of the crossbar. Ghazal could not have crawled under it, for a horse will never do that, but he had used the top of his head to work the bar upward until it fell over against the wall.

Marzuki ordered horses saddled for us, and we set off down the avenue leading from Amrieh to the hills, where we encountered a group of Bedouins who told us that they had seen a chestnut horse pursued by two riders.

Within half a mile from Amrieh we turned off into the desert and soon came across Arab herdsmen with their pasturing camels. They also had seen the horse.

"How far away?" we asked the herdsmen.

They pointed to the hill. "On the uplands just beyond."

We rode on, over the hill into a wide plain. At a little distance we saw two riderless horses, tails flying high over their backs, one a chestnut stallion, and the other a dapple-grey mare. Two men following them were trying in vain to separate the chestnut and his companion, for they were plunging and kicking vigorously.

Marzuki and I closed in from the opposite side. The chestnut—undoubtedly it was Ghazal—still ran at full speed behind the grey mare. She turned upon him, squealing and kicking in an attempt to fight him off. And again both ran away, manes and tails high.

They led us toward the edge of the plain, with the sun behind us. The wind blew hard across the gravel tableland. Hills rose to the south, and a gradual slope to the north.

55

The grey mare was no less fleet-footed than Ghazal, though more compact and rounded of line. They capered with the verve of two giddy foals, now swiftly speeding along, now with quick, short turns trying to waylay each other.

Marzuki leaned forward in his saddle and signaled me to follow him.

With the aid of another man, we almost succeeded in separating Ghazal and his mate, but the stallion turned and held off Marzuki's horse, roaring and pawing the ground before him.

The mare came on flying hoofs toward Ghazal, lightly touching his croup as she passed him. With a squeal he whirled about and followed her toward a rise in the ground where we lost sight of them. When they reappeared, the giddy little mare, lost in love of Ghazal, was following obediently at his heels.

Now it was easy to separate them. Marzuki and I took the grey mare between our horses, never losing touch of her in spite of her uneasiness.

In an effort to return to the side of his mare, Ghazal almost vaulted over Marzuki's horse. I cried to Ghazal; he pricked up his ears at the sound of my voice and came in full gallop toward me. I started my horse on a run in the opposite direction to draw him away from Marzuki's and the grey mare, but he raced madly past me.

When I dismounted, he watched me curiously with the gentle gaze of his large eyes, and his ears switched in lively play. The flame was still there, but subdued and calm.

Only after I scolded Ghazal, did I allow him to step closer. His nose carefully searched over me until he found his favorite spot, the pit under my left shoulder, where he snorted contentedly, inhaling my friendly scent—the sign of his surrender.

The owner of the little grey mare was Rashayd, a Bedouin of eastern Arabia. I learned that he had been on a political mission to the border of Tripoli and belonged to the same secret Arabian society as Marzuki. He looked very barbaric with his crown of braided lovelocks and his dark red beard, pointed and curly like a swashbuckling d'Artagnan's. He was about thirty and only of medium height. Spare, as all desert people are, with hawklike features and merry eye, his broad smile flashed white in his swarthy face.

Rashayd asked to accompany us to Alexandria, as Marzuki and I planned to leave Amrieh next day.

In the early afternoon we started, riding parallel to the sea and the railroad line. The desert hills were barren, but in valleys near the ocean were rolling green meadows with great flocks of sheep.

Rashayd's grey mare, Wudiyeh (the white antelope) could well compare in quality with Ghazal. Small, too, she was, but also deep in chest, with a short back, and level, long hindquarters, carrying her tail beautifully. There were more fine details in her lean wedge-shaped head, but she, too, was emaciated—the result of long rides and scanty food. Bedouins of inner Arabia ride only mares on raids and other long excursions because the temperament of mares is quieter and they do not betray themselves by neighing. In Egypt, however, where there is no raiding such as that in the Arabian desert, the natives mount stallions.

As we rode along, Ghazal and Wudiyeh kept on playing with each other. Wudiyeh's favorite trick was to rub the top of her head under Ghazal's neck and then jab him with her knees. But Ghazal in turn found an opportune moment to take gentle revenge on his friend. We had to keep our eyes constantly on the two horses.

That night we stayed in a nomad camp where Marzuki had left one of his race camels. The caretaker was an old friend of Marzuki, an Arab from the Sudan. He had grown rich years before, trading in slaves, ivory, and ostrich plumes. The pride of his heart was a stuffed, seven-foot crocodile with red-glass eyes. Gold tassels hung from its teeth—amulets which the old man sold to the superstitious natives.

Though reputed to be ninety-three years old, the Arab went out with us the next morning on his mare to a pasture to find Marzuki's race camel. Named after an ancient heroic maiden of the Ruala tribe, Alia was as beautiful a dhalul (race camel) as Marzuki had described her to be, but no one now dared to ride this lovely she-camel. She had been stained by the blood of her slaughtered owner, whom the Shammar Bedouins had killed on her back. Rashayd had inherited Alia, but as he believed in the superstitions of his people, he would not ride her. I, however, was not superstitious, and bought her for thirty-five gold pounds.

Alia was exquisite, not only by reason of her big dark eyes but also because of her elegantly slender shape—so like a deer's—and her soft fawn-colored coat which never lost its luster. She possessed all the points of the ideal dhalul, and even Rashayd hailed her as one of the finest she-camels among the Ruala tribes. Like the best in Arabia, she was a daughter of the Shararat. Her parents were thoroughbreds.

"She hath a lion's head with gazelle eyes," Rashayd told me while he pointed out to me the perfect line that speaks for speed and lightness of motion—the high-swung belly-line

58

from the breastbone to the hind thighs, the sharp slope from the hump to the tail, the straight drop of the hocks and hind-feet. This racing build gave her perfect freedom.

Had she faults? If so, I do not know them. Her senses were flawless—sharp eyes, alert hearing, good scent. Her disposition was gentle, and her gait so even and quiet that one could go to sleep on her saddle. She was quiet at saddling and did not shy. Her speed was like that of an ostrich.

I was happy to own Alia and quickly set about acquainting her with Ghazal. Miraculously he was not jealous but took a great liking to her. Perhaps he knew already that I could never love anyone as I loved him.

Poor little Alia had been neglected since her master's death. She craved attention. She stretched her immense neck backward to pull on my sleves or to touch my hand with her soft nose.

I rode Alia with Ghazal tied to her saddle by his halter rope, or with Rashayd sitting behind my camel saddle, leading Ghazal. In the evening I leaned against Alia's body, and when she reached around, I felt her warm breath, sweet with the fragrance of thyme and camomile.

Alia conversed with me in her own way, with speaking eyes and a touch of her lips against my foot to indicate that she wanted me to shift my position on her saddle. Her throaty voice was capable of plaintive noises, but I discovered that even her most querulous sounds were not meant to be complaints.

Every morning I tied Ghazal to the girth of my camel saddle, and we were off—Ghazal with that swift, bounding stride of the led-horse. Noiselessly we trailed along. The lustrous eyes of Alia searched the distance; the little silver chains around her face tinkled softly; the long tassels of the saddle-covers flapped under her belly, back and forth, back and forth. Her long slender neck bobbed up and down like the prow of a good ship breasting the waves. . . .

I was accustomed by now to Alia's easy stride. The strenuous exercise of camel riding had been difficult for me in the beginning. The pitching and shaking one gets in a long, fast pace requires firm muscles of the back and abdomen. The North African Arab winds yards of sash tightly around his waist in order to brace himself against the pounding, pile-driving motion of the camel's legs. The Ruala and other men of Arabian tribes leave free play to their muscles from the shoulders to the hips and, therefore, have more elastic figures than their African brothers.

Marzuki always rode in front of us, his gaunt camel looking at times like an ostrich as it sped over the plain. The deception was even greater when his animal trotted. Then each pair of saddlebags rose rhythmically and flapped back to the shoulders of the camel like the wings of a great bird, and the fringes fluttering in the wind were like trembling plumes or downy feathers.

There is no more comfortable method of travel than in an Arabian camel saddle. A taut leather skin is stretched over the wooden tree to form a seat between the high pommel in front and the high cantle behind. Quilted pads cover the skirt, seat, and flaps of the saddle. For greater comfort, blankets and ornamented leather covers are thrown over it, and finally three sheepskins which are used by night as bedding on the ground.

The huge camel saddlebags on both sides of the animals are deep enough to carry a grown person in comfort, and nothing induces sleep more certainly than the softly swaying pace of a highbred camel.

60

Rashayd had to leave us now and go on by another road to Kantara, on the Suez Canal, and beyond through the Sinai to the Gulf of Akaba. A rainstorm overtook us with a burst of hail before we parted from him. Marzuki called it a good omen, but I saw only that we were thoroughly soaked and must change clothing. However, he and Rashayd seemed in no way bothered.

We were sorry to say farewell to our friend and his dapple-grey mare. I had grown very fond of Rashayd. Although he was a fighting man, lacking Marzuki's gentleness, he was loyal and had a vigorous sense of humor. Above all, Rashayd was a man of nature who treated animals as if they were his children, dealing sympathetically with their changing moods.

I would have given anything to own his mare, but he loved Wudiyeh too much to part with her. She was the most precious of Rashayd's possessions.

He would not say farewell until I had promised to see him again. Lest I give my word merely in jest, he picked a withered stalk and made me swear by the life which had once been within it that, if I journeyed to Arabia, I would look for him among the Ruala tribe.

When Marzuki and I reached home, Charlotte gave us a note which had arrived from Sheykh Ammer during our absence. It informed us that—everything going well—he would meet us in Arabia. He also included addresses of friends, one in Hamma and another in Damascus.

"These friends," he wrote, "will bring you in safety to my home in the Hamad desert." And he bestowed upon me the name of Aziz. Although Bedouins are not accustomed to betray emotion, Marzuki had difficulty in finishing the letter, so affected was he. Aziz, he explained, was the name of Sheykh Ammer's son—a boy of seventeen—who had been killed in the Tripoli War. My friends had never before spoken to me of this tragic loss. After Marzuki had left the room, there was a moment of silence. Then Charlotte said softly, "Aziz, I can't help feeling that there is a destiny behind your going to Arabia, and I know you will come back, so I won't mind staying here alone to take care of our little place."

Far into the night we discussed the future.

Charlotte, though not yet seventeen, had the wisdom of maturity. I felt safe leaving her among our good friends. She had a spirit of happiness and they all loved her.

5

TWO WEEKS LATER Marzuki and I loaded Ghazal and Nahr (a bay Arabian stallion), and our camels, Alia and Rimeh (Marzuki's dhalul), into the train for Salhiyeh. On the following day we rode to Kantara, then crossed the Suez Canal, and camped on Tell es-Samut with Bedouins from the Sinai.

We reached the Palestine border in five easy stages, were held for a day in the quarantine station at el'Arish, and arrived in Jerusalem on a Sabbath, dust-covered and weary. But the sight of the Mount of Olives with the great spire of the Russian Church of the Ascension gleaming at its summit refreshed us. We rode into the valley of Hinnom with the domes and minarets of the temple place and the ancient walls of Zion before us.

Our host during the eleven-day stay was a friend, a Jewish doctor, who owned a garden place with a fine stable near Rephaim. We left the Holy City with memories not only of the places we had visited, but of the people we had met— the Jewish family who were so gracious to us in Jerusalem, and the friendly Franciscan friar, our companion and guide on the ride to the River Jordan and the Dead Sea.

On our five-day ride to Mount Carmel and Haifa, Marzuki and I lived like medieval pilgrims, finding shelter in Latin monasteries and at a Maltese hospice. Our meals we ate by the wayside—once under a votive tree hung with sacrificial offerings, and another time at Jacob's Well, where Jesus had met the woman of Samaria. . . .

The journey was a dreamlike passage under sunny skies. The loveliest spot of all was Nazareth with its white houses and terraced gardens set in the folds of green hills. Its tumbled rock walls were gay with purple poppies, and flocks of sheep browsed in the meadows. A little shepherd boy stood beside his mother near the well of Mary. He might have been the son of Miriam, innocent, in love with the hills and the fragrance of the flowers. He drew water from the well, the only spring near Nazareth, and helped his mother carry the heavy pitcher to their home.

The plain of Esdraelon lay before us. And though snow-capped Mt. Hermon beckoned us from beyond the Syrian border, we followed the coast past Acre and Saida to Beyrouth.

Beyrouth to Damascus! Many times I have since made this journey, by carriage, automobile, train, and on horseback. But it has never been so exciting as that first time when Ghazal and Alia were with me and Marzuki rode at my side.

From the semitropical gardens of Beyrouth we climbed a winding road past pine forests and Syrian villages to the snow-covered rose-hued summits of the Lebanon mountains and beyond, to quaint old Zahleh, the Beka plains, and the Anti-Lebanon mountains.

Marzuki led me to a little-used road on a barren hillside from which I had my first view of Damascus, city of the Omayyades, extolled by the Arabian poets as the paradise of the world. Seen from above, it is a fresh green leaf fallen into the brown desert. A hundred little streams of the Barada River spread out like veins. The lowlands are rich with fruit and flowers, and the air is compounded of desert sun and wind that has known snow.

Once in the city, Marzuki and I, mounted on our horses, made the rounds of the bazaars, through narrow winding lanes of the native quarters, past open, cobbled squares with plane trees and splashing fountains. No one pushed us aside in the crowded streets, but many laid their hands upon Ghazal, exclaiming, "Masha'llah."

The bazaars of Damascus gave me at once a feeling—which I had never had in Cairo—that I was very near to the desert with its caravans and the Bedouins. The very air of Damascus breathed with fragrant perfumes of the desert, and unveiled women from the tribes walked through the market lanes.

Into the bazaar of the saddle-makers crowded nomad Arabs, mounted on their camels and horses. The entrances to the stalls of the merchants were bedecked with colorful Arabian bridles and Syrian saddles and blankets.

At one end of the silk bazaar, near the mosque of the Omayyades, Marzuki knew of an old Arab café. We allowed Ghazal and Nahr to stand next to our table and chairs, by a marble fountain.

Birds were so tame that they perched on our table or on the iron grillwork of the fountain, whipping their tails and swishing across the basin to steal a few drops of water.

The solitude under the roof of green leaves was interrupted only by the arrival of some Bedouins from the desert. They had come to pray at the mosque. The men wore soft sandals, but their women clanked across the cobblestones like a platoon of Russian soldiers. Their boots were not only hobnailed but also had horseshoe-shaped solid iron heels with sharp edges almost an inch long. In villages and tent-camps the women do the heavy work, and it is all too easy to slip on the wet rim of a well and plunge to disaster.

Marzuki's relatives lived in the Maidan, where a market was held every week by the Agheyl, the horse and camel traders. Here in the Maidan the desert Bedouins met the white-turbaned Druses, and the fellahin faced the shepherds of the hills.

The Maidan of Damascus had come into existence only three or four generations ago and had grown rapidly with the development of the Medina Railway and the French line to Haifa, whose terminals were built at the southern end of the Maidan. The great pilgrimages to the holy cities, twelve hundred miles away in the Hejaz, used to start at this point.

How different was Damascus from Cairo. The bracing air of the desert highland and the people with ruddy cheeks were divorced by a whole world from the lowland of Egypt with its sluggish brown Nile and its slow, heavy-set natives.

In Damascus I knew I was among genuine Arabs. The air was that of desert Arabia, not Egypt or Northern Africa. I stood on the threshold of the "Island of the Arabs." Already its spaciousness had communicated itself to my consciousness. Was Damascus the gateway to my destiny?

Marzuki and I decided to join three Ruala Bedouins returning to the desert with purchases they had made in Damascus. Marzuki knew their chiefs, most important of whom were Prince Nuri Sha'lan and his son Nauaf. Indirectly, I, too, might claim friendship with the Ruala through Rashayd, whose mare had fallen so much in love with Ghazal in Amrieh.

The first rains had come three weeks before, and desert travel in such a season promised to be pleasant. At last I was to go into the true Arabian desert.

66

Wudiyeh—War Mare of the Desert

UNDER A BLUE and cloudless sky we left the city I so loved. Summer still hung in the air, but away in the distance winter had already touched the Lebanon with fresh snow. As we rode past the walnut orchards and olive groves of Damascus, my heart was filled with sadness. Never before had this feeling possessed me so strongly. It came upon me suddenly that this was the last station of my small world and that I was setting out to cross a new ocean to an unknown shore. For the first time the question of the unknown frightened me.

We had no compass and no map. At that time desert Arabia had not been charted. True, Marzuki accompanied me and he knew the desert. And I had Ghazal who had come from this part of the world. But still I felt oddly disquieted.

We were in strange company—three old men and three old women, small figures, weatherworn and almost in rags, riding on fine-boned camels. One blue-grey mare was led by her halter rope. Three old men, three old women, five camels and a mare. One woman rode alone, as did one man; but the others traveled in pairs, the women behind their men on the high camel saddles.

They were of the Ruala, members of one of the greatest tribes of the desert. They were rich in camels and had larger tents than the other Arabs, and were wealthy according to desert standards. They roamed from one end of Arabia to the other, raiding from Aleppo to the Persian Gulf, from the Hejaz to the Euphrates and Tigris. Their pasture districts extended for eleven hundred miles from Tudmor (Palmyra) through to the Nufud, the Red Sea desert to Tayma and Khaybar. They had strong allies, and many smaller tribes and village people in Central Arabia and Syria paid tribute to them. Sheykh Ammer and other Wuld Ali chiefs were their trusted friends, and the principal families had intermarried for ages past. The Prince of Riyadh, the Wahhabi leader Ibn Sa'ud, was of their blood.

I had thrown in my lot with outcasts of society—with men who raided other tribes for horses and camels. Was this not thievery? My own people and friends among the Damascenes had warned me. But Marzuki had kept up my spirits, and Ghazal and Alia had turned their soft gaze upon me in reassurance.

The old women, perched high on their camel saddles, waved their riding sticks and lightly touched the necks of their animals. They were full of laughter, the men began to sing and yodel. It all sounded very strange, and yet it was beautiful. They were riding homeward. They had left the city behind with all its trickeries and artificial comfort. Soon they would have to tighten their belts and forget that false paradise on the Barada River.

A little stream of water ran along the side of the road as we left Damascus. Abruptly it stopped. "Stay!" it seemed to warn me. The bright gardens and blue smoke drifting from adobe huts behind called, "You will miss us." The Bedouins swung their crops, their high-legged mounts went into longer strides.

"Marzuki!" I cried.

He looked back and saw me dismount and lead Ghazal back to the little stream and the last patch of green.

"Aziz!" he shouted to me. It was a command.

I felt like a child who had been caught cheating. Taking hold of Ghazal's mane, I remounted.

A fresh breeze sprang up and carried a melancholy whistle to me. Was that Marzuki mocking me for being such a coward? "That lucky devil," I said under my breath. "Going home."

I liked him; courage was as much a part of him as his lined, brown face and his merry eyes. As I came closer to him, I thought I heard him whistle again. But now the sound seemed to be lifted high into the air, returning to me like the echo of a song. I joined him. Marzuki was talking to his horse; from the air came the wild song of a bird.

"I thought it was your whistle, Marzuki," I said sheepishly.

"No, he is a friend come to bid you welcome to the desert. He came with the breeze. He is the desert lark with the speckled breast, and he always has his little mate with him."

Suddenly I felt free. Gone was my homesickness. I urged Marzuki into a gallop to join our camel riders. The old men and women were part of this great expanse on their light-footed, swaying camels. So was the poor little blue-grey mare, who hardly lifted her legs. Like pendulum rods they moved along without wasting any knee-action. Seeing us come, one of the old fellows made room in the saddle for his wife, who had been crouched behind the cantle, leading the blue-grey mare. He jumped onto the bare back of his rag-gedy old horse, gathering the rope in his hands, and chal-lenged Ghazal to a race.

As we went off, I wondered how the man could trust himself to this skeleton. But from the very moment that he landed on her back, she became transformed, taking on a gallantry all her own. She looked amazingly racy and noble as she gathered herself with the rider upon her withers. She carried her tail proudly and set her little hoofs lightly and sure-footedly as a young gazelle.

For a while we held our own. But soon the grey mare got away. This should not be. Ghazal was now in better shape than he had been in Egypt. I leaned forward, laid my hand upon his mane, and cried, "Ghazali!"

He answered with a loud neigh. He knew I wanted him to be serious. His hoofs drummed faster and faster over the hard gravel soil. Small stones peppered him as we came up to the grey mare. Side by side we raced with the yelling old man. The mare snorted, and laid back her ears. Her rider slid like a monkey back and forth, never touching the mare with his hands, though sometimes his naked feet knocked against her ribs.

Ghazal's hoofs beat in the same wild rhythm as the mare's, but he could not overtake her, no matter how hard he tried. For ten minutes or more there was no gain, then slowly the mare drew away, with her old rider shouting and laughing at us. The Rueyli and his blue-grey mare had won the race.

I dismounted. Ghazal shook himself and coughed, while I loosened his girth. The old man rode over. His mare gave not a sound. Only her thin nostrils dilated, and she trembled slightly. The horses sniffed at each other; Ghazal squealed a bit with jealousy and thrust his knee into her shoulder.

"She blows like a feather over the ground," her owner said with justifiable pride. And with a gesture of contempt, he added, "A dhaker—male—will never do. You must ride an entha—female. A stallion can never be a war horse."

"This dhaker *is* a war horse," Marzuki interrupted, and he told us of Ghazal's experience with Aziz, the son of Sheykh Ammer, who had used Ghazal in African Tripoli against the Italians. I had never heard it before.

To his companions, who now rode up on their camels, the old man repeated the story of Ghazal, and told how Aziz rode him to attack the enemies. They all dismounted to look at my horse.

"Masha'llah," they exclaimed in wonder, and asked Marzuki many questions about Ghazal and Aziz. They blessed Ghazal, and the old man laid his hand on my horse's forehead.

"Indeed he is asil—noble," Marzuki said with reverence of Ghazal. "Sire and dam are of the same strain, the Kuhaylan al-Krush."

Skirting Adra, the last outpost of civilization, we rode through a pass between two low hills, out into the Hamad, the rising high plateau-like land, which embraces the whole of northern Arabia. Within four hundred miles in each direction not a single well can be found, Marzuki informed me.

The nomads in this region depend entirely on rain pools and the pastures they find among undulating plains. If the rains fail altogether, the Bedouins and their vast herds of camels migrate to the neighborhood of the Euphrates and Tigris, or to the great depression of Wadi Sirhan and the cultivated land of Syria and Transjordan. Camel breeders do not fear the waterless stretches of the desert as the sheep- and goat-raising Arabs do, and for that reason camel owners alone remain independent and free.

We turned south from the shepherd hills into the camel

pastures of the Ruala. The third day out we overtook the pack camels of our Ruala companions. The animals and their drivers had been sent from Damascus several days before our own departure. Now we could not ride more than thirty miles a day, for we planned to remain with our friendly hosts.

Each day I liked them better. They were selfless people, trusting and childlike. Although these nomads had no learning, as we know it, their memories were tablets on which were graven the lore and ethics of their ancestors. Only that which was worth passing on to their children did they *add* to their store of knowledge. In this they were very unlike the Europeans who know too much for contentment, whose hearts are confused. *Their* minds were unburdened.

"An idea too complex to fit into poetry is of no value to remember," was a classic remark of the old Rueyli with the blue-grey mare.

These people had a natural ease and a noble bearing unrelated to their ragged garb. In spite of old garments and wrinkled faces they were aristocrats with noble features and fine bones, as were their haggard little horses and gaunt camels. The blue mare was covered with scars, and her coat was as ragged as her master's. But like him, she had unbelievable endurance. The old Rueyli was devoted to her. "I bathe her with tears of joy every morning," he told me, "the light of my life, the enriching one."

Her qualities were not striking beauty and physical perfection, such as I had seen in stone in Greece, nor did the little mare resemble even remotely the ideal picture of Phili in the old stained oaken frame above my bed. There were other degrees of excellence which these Bedouins loved in their horses—traits of almost sentimental and spiritual values. They esteemed their horses for intimate associations with

72

certain personal events—which might have happened on a raid or because of a love affair or a blood feud—in which the little mare was exchanged as a gift or a prize, and consequently forever regarded as a precious possession, or a token of love and peace.

I began to learn from them that there were other qualities in a horse than just a handsome shape and a noble carriage.

We bedded ourselves near our warm animals at night and did not sleep in thatch-roofed caravansaries, which housed vermin, mangy hounds, and thieves. The starlit sky was our roof, and the air we breathed was the clean breath of the desert.

Whenever we came to rest, the coffeepots were brought out. A fire blazed, and soon the bitter brew was handed to us. My companions did not mind going hungry if they had a few sips of coffee before falling off to sleep.

But most of the time we had plenty to eat. Pintail grouse—clouds of them—swept toward the earth to fall upon it like spattering hail. We found bustards, the famous hubara of the Arabs—turkey-like birds.

There was no road. We followed our own winding way through the wilderness. Its rusty soil and spare herbage would be cheerless to a traveler longing for lush meadows. Up and down we rode, the changless horizon calling to us. Depressions were touched with a breath of green, but the barren crest glimmered always with a sheen of fine gravel. Miraculously each hill and dale bore a name.

The wide hollows were blessed with rain pools, sometimes as big as a lake, though only a foot or two in depth. Our animals splashed through, stopping to drink greedily from the middle where the water was deepest and sweetest.

We found the carcasses of animals, weeks dead. Three rocks upon a pile of earth marked the grave of a woman whose hearthstones had been left with her as a tribute to her housewifely virtues. The old Rueyli told us that many Bedouins and their camels had perished in the drought before the rainy season.

A rainstorm visited us one afternoon. That night we built a fire of sweet-smelling herbs and tiny twigs and held our wet robes over the flame. When we were dry, we curled up close to our animals to sleep. From a distant rise in the plains a hyena cried like a lost child. It was not a reassuring sound.

I saw no trees, only small feathery shrubs. Marzuki said that there would be none until we reached Wadi Sirhan and the Nufud, the Red Sand Desert in the distant south.

My companions found the tracks of marauding parties and explained to me that they were tracks of camels with horses tied to their saddle cinches, coming from the south. "They are our own people," the Ruala told me proudly. "They lie in wait for the flocks of the Fid'an and Saba' near the shepherd hills."

To plunder sheep and camels was no crime, but a game with inviolate rules, a diversion in which the young bloods and the expert old riders tried their skill at the start of the rainy season. To belong to a party of spoilers, and scrupulously to protect women and children at the same time, was held an honor.

When our animals moved along in swift strides and the sun shone upon us from a cloudless sky, the old Rueyli was happiest. "Let us drink smoke," he said to Marzuki, who then filled his own pipe, a homemade instrument fashioned from a streaked lava rock.

It was a merry ride. The centuries were turned back;

Egypt and Europe no longer existed. More and more I became enamoured of the spaciousness of this nomadic world and of the beautiful imagery reflected in the soul of its people.

The desert held magic for my comrades. They did not worry, for they had long ago decided that God settles everything. Lacking the fanatic superstition of the African Arabs, they lived not by a religion, but by their faith. They did not bother with outward forms and rituals.

They told me much of the history and pedigrees of their horses, camels, and greyhounds, and always in words of poetry. Symbols fell unconsciously from the lips of these wandering Arabs, for eloquence, their only medium of expression, is their great gift, and their language is rich with meaning.

The old men—not one of whom could have been less than seventy—were covered with scars. They admitted that very few Bedouins live to such an age in the desert. Men perish in raids and hunts and accidents before the age of forty, and a sick person stands little chance of survival. The migration goes on. There is no time to care for the weak; they must fall by the wayside. As fatalists, they expect and prefer such a death to a lingering illness, although disease is rare in the desert.

The blue mare grew daily more emaciated. An abscess developed on her chest from an infection suffered in Damascus. One evening the old man fired her with a piece of hot iron. She lost much blood, and I believed that she could not possibly go on with us. But next day she pranced around like a young foal, apparently relieved of great pain. That night she outgalloped and outwitted a hare which her master stirred up in some small camel grass.

In Damascus I had bought some expensive Bedouin cloaks,

conventional gifts to present to Prince Nuri Sha'lan and his son. But Marzuki warned me that the matter of gifts was a complicated affair in Arabia. The best plan would be to bring no presents, but to arrive poor as beggars.

"If we arrive as kings," Marzuki added, "we shall leave as beggars. Our hosts will show affection for our possessions to such a degree that we shall be forced to give them away."

"They will not covet our horses," Marzuki reassured me when I looked anxiously at Ghazal. "But let us come poor, and thus neither offend nor oblige any of the great chiefs."

I saw the logic of that, and thought awhile. "Let us give the cloaks to our companions. They deserve them," I said.

"No," Marzuki said. "Tomorrow, after sunrise, we shall ride ahead of our friends and throw these cloaks away. The old men will find them and try to return them to us, but we shall say that we have no need of these things. Thus no one can say that we have made presents to our companions and none to Nuri and the great chiefs."

My mind was awhirl with these intricate desert ethics. But I could not help admiring Marzuki's ingenuity.

His plan worked well. We dropped the gold embroidered cloaks and silk handkerchiefs, and our friends picked them up. When they brought the "lost articles" to us, we showed surprise. "Why, we threw them away! We do not wish to insult Nuri with such lowly gifts."

"Ah, but they will do for us," they cried.

That was exactly what we wanted to hear. "Surely, take them if you want them," I said, dismissing them with a gesture.

2

LATE IN THE afternoon of our seventh day, near the foothills of the volcanic desert, we sighted a column of dhalul suddenly emerging from a depression. Spying us, the riders dismounted at once from their camels and took to their horses to attack us. We had no time left to try an escape; the country was rough and hard-going with heavy sand and protruding rocks. The group of mounted men bore down upon us in a wild dash. A cloud of dust whirled up from the hoofs of their mounts, enveloping us as the riders drew rein. Bearded faces, gleaming guns, the heads of excited horses appeared through the clearing dust. With rifles propped against their thighs, the riders (about twenty of them) sat motionless before us. I drew Ghazal to an uneasy halt.

A single man on a powerful jet-black Syrian stallion rode towards us. He was middle-aged, tall and thick-set, dressed in gaudy garments with a black shepherd coat flung over his shoulders. On his lap he held a heavy, silver-mounted gun. He stopped a few feet from us to view our group with critical eyes, saying not a word. Two wolflike dogs trailed among the horses, finally taking positions beside the rider.

Raising his hand, Marzuki called to the leader, "As-Salam'-Alayk—peace be with you!"

"As-Sam'Alayk—death be with you!" the man thundered back.

It was a play of words—as-sam instead of as-salam—and there was only one man who dared to greet friends and foe alike with this infidel mockery. He was Abu-Barakish, the traitor, whom the natives of the desert border districts knew well, for he had taken bribes from both the Druses and the Turks. In consequence he had been nicknamed Barakish, after the fabulous bird of Moslem legend which changes the color of its plumage at will.

We had been forewarned that we might encounter him, as the blackguard's raiding parties extended to the east of the Harra (volcanic) desert. The Turks had put a price on his head, branding him "As-Saffah" (the bloody one)—only one of many unflattering titles of which, perversely, he was proud. His band of outlaws, originally numbering more than seventy men, had dwindled. Living by robbery and murder, they made the most out of their country's distressing plight.

"As-*Sam* or As-*Salam*," Mazurki said to the raider, "they mean nothing to you, but God weighs such words on our tongues."

"Akhu-Atika has no dealings with God," the leader responded with a coarse laugh.

Akhu-Atika (brother of Atika) he called himself. His sister was said to resemble the historic Atika, a female Bluebeard who had done away with three or four husbands. The proud brother of such a sister would not grant us much grace.

He dug the knifelike edges of his Syrian stirrups into his black stallion. The horse squealed and leapt forward, almost knocking over Ghazal and Alia as he bounded into us. Growling and yelping, the dogs also jumped at us. Alia plunged away.

With a loud cry Ghazal rose on his hindfeet and struck a vicious blow upon the shoulder of the black horse, barely

78

missing the rider's leg. Fiercely he tore into the midst of the raiders, lashing out with his hoofs, grunting with madness, trying to break through the defense of his enemies. But the raiders were pressing in upon us, overwhelming us. I felt a sharp blow on my head, and, as I was torn from Ghazal, the world went black . . . .

When I awoke I found myself upon the ground. It was night. Above me curled the smoke of an open fire. Flames shot through the grey pennant of smoke, like the pains shooting through my body. Strange sounds of men and animals came to me, and the pungent odor of camel-dung fires. I thought of Ghazal—and of Alia—and of Marzuki—and our companions.

Finally I heard Marzuki speak, but I could not see him, nor understand his words. With difficulty I raised myself upon my elbow. Men were squatting around the fires, and I saw the familiar figures of the old men and women of the Ruala not far away, talking to the chief, Abu-Barakish. My gaze wandered from them, out to the horses and camels scattered along the fringe of the camp, until I found Marzuki with Ghazal and Alia.

When they realized that I conscious, Marzuki and Abu-Barakish came and sat down at my side. Abu-Barakish ordered camel saddles to be brought and placed on the ground, so that we might lean against them.

"He is your servant?" Abu-Barakish asked me, regarding Marzuki.

"No, Marzuki is a poet, a seer," I answered.

To the Arabs the gift of poetry is a spiritual one, and much respect is paid to such men.

"Let the man recite some of his poems," the chief commanded.

"Your Excellency," Marzuki answered (but it sounded suspiciously like a mockery), "I have already composed one in your honor."

"Only after death should homage be given a man," the bandit answered pompously.

"Perhaps you of all men deserve a song before you die," Marzuki replied.

"Before I die?" asked the chief.

"There may be none to sing your praises after you are dead," Marzuki ventured impudently.

"Remove this man," ordered the chief, and a dozen arms reached out to pull Marzuki away.

"Leave him, Akhu-Atika," I warned. "Marzuki is not an ordinary man. He may be of great value to you some day."

"Could he do us a service among the tribes?" the renegade asked sharply.

Marzuki was allowed to drop to his seat again, and the chief began to explain why our lives had been spared. It appeared that Akhu-Atika needed us for a definite purpose. My first thought was that he was going to hold us for ransom, and dispatch a member of the band to Syria for the money.

"We have no friends in Syria any more," he said, answering my thought. "Jauf would be a much safer country for us. There are no blood feuds against us there. We have heard, too, that Nuri's son, Nauaf, needs men like us to help him conquer Ibn Rashid's government in Jauf."

What he said was true. Nauaf was fighting at Jauf and needed more soldiers. The bandit and his desperadoes might be a welcome addition to Nauaf and Nuri's forces.

80

"You are a Nasrani?" he asked me abruptly. Nasrani (Nazarene) is the contemptuous term for a Christian.

"I am a Missihi—one who awaits the Messiah," I replied.

"Let us not discuss religion," he broke in. "You are not a Moslem; that is all I want to know. You shall do me a favor."

"I hope your wish can be fulfilled easily, Akhu-Atika," I answered politely.

"Do not call me Akhu-Atika any more," he begged. "Call me by my real name—Ali ibn Ma'sum."

"Then let us say, 'Peace be with you,' Ali ibn Ma'sum," I suggested.

The big man smiled at my insistent demand for the word 'peace' and said, "Since you desire to hear it from my lips I will pronounce it to you, 'As-Salam Alayk.'"

I repeated the word, and Marzuki, too, was assured with the salutation of peace. Though these men were robbers, the word of peace might go a long way with them.

Now I asked him what favor it was I could do for him. With a gesture he waved my question aside and persuaded me to eat first. As I ate, he leaned over my shoulder and whispered, "A Nasrani should not ride a horse of such noble breeding among Believers. I will buy your stallion."

I ignored his insult and answered him quietly, "Ghazal has only been lent to me by Sheykh Ammer. And in any case my horse would not allow a stranger to mount him."

Akhu-Atika turned to his men and asked boisterously, "Does a horse exist that I could not ride?"

They looked at one another with strange expressions on their faces, but they all assured him volubly that such a horse did not exist.

"At sunrise you will let me ride your stallion," the braggart boasted.

All through the night I heard his loud voice talking boastfully to his men. In the morning I found I had fallen prey to wild fears of this man whose mere touch I knew Ghazal would resent. . . . The barking dogs and the circle of long-robed men in discussion with their chief reminded me that we were still prisoners of Akhu-Atika's raiding party. I borrowed Marzuki's camel wand. Slender though it was, it might be a weapon against the vicious dogs.

Ghazal's eyes watched me as I walked over to the rise of a sand dune. I chose a spot below its curved ridge, the siyuf (scimitar), the Arabs call it. A thin veil of sand floated over my head without a solitary grain touching me. It drifted constantly from the ledge to the ground below, mysteriously creating a new dune. This crescent-shaped wave of sand was as much a nomad as the Bedu, who roam the desert's jealously guarded emptiness. The small breeze, the unseen one, would hasten its migration. I heard its voice about me. Since that hour I have felt that perhaps I might understand the message of the desert. I threw myself upon its soft bed, lost in dreams. As I rose from the sand dune, I saw Alia standing against the sun in a halo of golden light. Her head was raised high, she watched me intently and in silence. I felt that she had been there a long while. As I neared her, she bleatedly feebly. It was an anxious cry. When I reached out my hand to stroke her, to lead the timid animal back to our fold, I heard a shout behind us. A guard, whose presence I had not suspected, stepped forward with his gun and ordered me to return to the chief.

Akhu-Atika was not in a pleasant mood. His angry words to me were in sharp contrast to his polite behavior of the night before. Straightaway he ordered me to put his clumsy Syrian saddle upon Ghazal. I wanted to refuse but decided to do as I was told. It would be better to make a speedy end of his mockery.

The big jet-black Syrian (Druse) stallion had already been saddled. He stood at least four inches taller than Ghazal—a powerful horse, handsome in his own way, but his tail fell away abruptly from the slanting hipbone towards his hocks. His neck also lacked the graceful curve of the Arabian. His head was rather narrow and flat, with small eyes set high, and I missed the intelligent and gentle expression of the true desert horse.

The saddle trappings and bridle I had to put on Ghazal were elaborate, fit rather for a fantasia of village Arabs. The shashiya, or riding pad, was of gold brocade, and the head-stall ornamented with silver and gold inlay.

After I had shown Ghazal under the saddle, and had demonstrated how easy it really was to handle him, the chief brusquely ordered me to dismount. As he approached and tried to lay his hand on Ghazal, my horse snorted a warning and drew away from him. Only because of my interference did Ghazal finally allow the chief to touch him and seat himself on his back. Akhu-Atika should have seen that the horse was only putting a good face on a bad game. I warned him to handle Ghazal gently, but he, overbearing and confident of his own horsemanship, brushed me impatiently aside and spurred Ghazal's flanks with the sharp edges of his stirrups. With a loud cry, Ghazal leaped forward, almost unseating the man on his back. Akhu-Atika cried out to his henchman, who raced behind him on the black stallion, gathered the whip in his hand, and lashed out, dealing a frightful blow across Ghazal's croup.

For a moment I was stunned. Ghazal galloped away at a mad speed, the Syrian stallion and his rider on his heels.

Suddenly Ghazal threw himself straight into the air, and as he plunged backward, Akhu-Atika was hurled from the saddle and crushed under Ghazal's body.

Dust still enveloped the scene as Ghazal struggled to free himself of the entangling saddle trappings and the human body.

The raiders carried their unconscious chief back to camp. His back broken, he expired without regaining consciousness. Some of the men tried to put the blame for the accident upon me; others, on the chief himself. However, all agreed that it was Ghazal who had killed Akhu-Atika and that no Moslem law punished an animal.

During these discussions our old women were burying Akhu-Atika in the hollow between the singing sand dune and her "daughter"—the newly formed hillock. The shattered tree of the saddle, minus the elaborate trappings, was placed over the chief's grave.

I heard Marzuki say, "The Author of Life decided that Akhu-Atika should die. His fate was tied about his neck. May Allah be kind to him and whiten his dark face on the day of judgment. May it shine like the bright countenance of the moon, the orb of night, the essence of all beauty and loveliness."

"Marzuki, the poet, is still with us," I said in jest.

Marzuki gave me a sly wink. "In death Akhu-Atika is greater than in life."

The new leader of the band discussed with Marzuki and the Ruala the plan of riding with us to Nuri's camp and joining with Nuri's son Nauaf in his fights near Jauf. Being still afraid of them, we unanimously accepted their company as the most graceful way out of our dilemma.

84

We were now riding directly east into the high plateau region of Jabal'Enaza. Here on the second day after leaving the volcanic desert, a solitary rider appeared. His actions at first seemed suspicious, but as he came closer, Marzuki rode empty-handed toward him. The two men dismounted and made signs to each other, and then Marzuki led the other back to us.

The stranger was a young Rueyli. After we had built a fire and had had coffee, the man talked. The Ruala, the youth told us, were only two days' ride away. Much rain had fallen in that region. The pastures were sweet and plentiful, and the main body of the tribe had moved into depressions east of Jabal'Enaza.

That night our visitor produced part of a gazelle, shot the day before. Hanging from his camel saddle, it had dried in the sun and sterile air. We roasted the venison, and set to it like hungry wolves. Ghazal stamped the earth and snorted.

"He is greedy," Marzuki laughed. "He envies us. Let him smell a bone."

I handed Ghazal a good piece of the meat. His teeth snapped into it like a trap. He munched it almost savagely. I could not believe my eyes.

"Masha'llah!" the men cried as they watched Ghazal tear one morsel after another from the leg of venison I held in my hand.

"Wallah—by God!" they shouted. "Thy horse is indeed a dog of the wilderness."

In the morning the wind whipped so fiercely about us that we could not build a fire, but nourished from last night's game, we were soon off in the early dawn. As the sun rose, we looked at each other with shouts of laughter. We were encrusted with fine brown dust, and our animals looked like ghosts.

All morning the storm swirled clouds of dust about us; then at noon a rain squall burst upon us, lasting for some hours. When the sun broke through, we tossed off our wet shepherd coats, and looked upon a radiant new world. Great puffs of clouds rode the sky, casting their shadows upon the smooth plain. From a dry wash between two far-stretching slopes came the sound of running hoofs. We stopped our animals and heard the scattering of gravel. Seven mares scrambled around the bend, manes flying.

I could hardly hold Ghazal, who wanted to fly with them. Marzuki had to dismount and hang on to his own stallion by the halter rope. The mares raced across the wash and up the other side. They spread out across the slope, panting and snorting, lashing their flanks with their tails and eyeing us curiously through tangled foretops.

None of us moved. The restless herd must not be disturbed. We spoke only with signs. Here and there along the slope shadows of men appeared, cautiously, for we might be enemies. Recognizing us, the shepherds came boldly nearer. While some went over to their mares and captured them by their manes, others approached us and spoke to the old Rueyli. The scent of our horses had been wafted to the mares pasturing peacefully around the bend of the wadi, and they had come to investigate. Thus we saw the first Ruala, but only a small clan. Another half day's ride still separated us from Nuri's large camp.

We stayed the night beside the cluster of black tents of our new-found acquaintances. The big brush fire in the hearth of a nearby tent was blazing hot. I marveled that the flames, which often reached to the ceiling, did not consume the shelter.

During the night it drizzled again, but it was clear in the morning. The floor of the old rain lake was slippery, and the hoofs of our horses accumulated mud until the animals seemed to walk with bricks for feet.

I felt no fear in this vast desert in the company of the Bedouins. The Bedouin does not stalk the wilderness alone; he needs the society of his fellow men. Each year he traverses his tribe's pasture districts with his clan from one end to the other and back again. He visits neighboring tribes, and raids the length and breadth of the land, but never alone. He knows the stars, not as an astronomer knows them, but as a man of the earth who has learned to read a few pictures in the constellations as they travel across the face of the night.

Next morning we reached the famous cairn of Jabal'Enaza —highest point in northern Arabia. On this upland I rested for hours, watching the strange world of light and shadow. Gradually I began to notice life. Migratory birds floated by like the shadow of a cloud. On a pale green sheen between two rolling hills moved fawn-colored spots—grazing camels. Black dots along the folds of the earth were black tents of the Ruala in the shelter of a low hill, looking like boulders along a wash. I made out the smoke of their fires, and as I sat blinking, shading my eyes with my hand, more camels appeared, and more Arab camps, hugging the warm skin of the earth.

I watched the breaking up of camps, the rolling of tent canvases and packing of provisions upon camel backs. Families were migrating again. This world, which at first sight had looked so barren, was fine pasture land, the watershed of northern Arabia.

When our pack camels drew near we mounted again and rode down into the luminous world.

All the morning we rode before we reached the camps that to me had seemed so close.

Armed men came to us and greeted us with shouts. "Strength!" they called—an invitation to enter their tents. We could have furnished excuses to proceed direct to Nuri's camp, but as our pack animals were trailing behind, cropping herbage, and as time has no meaning in Arabia, we could spend as many hours here as we chose. So we decided to ride to the nearest tent with one of the men.

"Ha," said our host, "you came to see Nuri." (He respected Nuri, but would not call him prince, because like his fellow Bedouins he believed in desert democracy.) "Wallah —by God—he is over there, half a day's ride away. Stay and let us talk; you will honor my house."

He took the headgear from our horses, hobbled their feet and hung the headstalls on the tent's center post.

The man had been wounded near Jauf and wore a bandage across his right shoulder. Enthusiastically our companions of the late Akhu-Atika's gang inquired about the possibility of joining Nauaf in his fight against the Shammar in Jauf.

"You are welcome," our host said. "Nauaf needs such brave allies as you."

Nauaf, so successful in the beginning, had been routed by superior forces of the Shammar and was retreating to his own migrating tribe. Due to his failure Nauaf drew upon himself the ire of his father, Nuri Sha'lan, who still saw no good for the Ruala in the adventures of his son. Frantically hiring new fighters among his own tribe and among the settlers in Syria, Nauaf planned again to ride with a much greater army of mounted men against Jauf.

Such were the political conditions in that part of the world, we learned, as we rested at this outlying camp of the great Ruala tribe. For political reasons, and also because of Nuri's position as supreme chief of the desert, Marzuki decided that it would be wise for him first to see Nuri alone and announce my arrival.

3

WHILE I WAITED two days for Marzuki's return, I gained some insight into the migratory life of this camel-breeding tribe of the Ruala. I felt overwhelmed, as if by the sudden vision of a mirage, as I looked over the barren wilderness with vast encampments sprawling beyond the range of vision and pasturing flocks spread out in all directions. Scattered across the desert, rose seven thousand tents, and thousands of camels, tens of thousands, were cropping the miniature plants. Never could I have imagined such a sight as these big congregations of camels, spreading out toward the rising land.

A miracle this was, numberless animals existing thus on almost invisible herbage. The camels and mares were now in splendid condition—their coats sleek and shining. Forgotten was the hunger of the previous weeks, for showers had filled the depression with rain water and pasture.

The nights in a nomad camp are calm in spite of the large flocks couched near the tents, but on the morning when Marzuki returned before dawn on his stallion, the dogs rushed out snarling and held him at bay, and the camels interrupted the chewing of their cuds to raise complaining groans. Our host was up on the instant to call the dogs away. He hobbled Marzuki's horse and tied him to a long rope on a tent stake. Meanwhile, other members of the household couched the restless camels. Water was set to boil, and we leaned on our camel saddles to discuss events.

Marzuki had seen Nuri. It was agreed that we would not leave before sunrise for the journey to Nuri's great tent, the most spacious in all Arabia.

What experience in the world could be like that of awakening before sunrise in a Bedouin tent, with a cheerful fire and Ghazal nickering a welcome to you? The air of the tent is warm, and you enjoy it greedily before you go out to greet your horse. The fragrance of his body comes to you as you push your hands under his covers to stroke his warm coat.

Our host wanted no thanks. He placed my camel saddle on Alia, and I said casually to him when I left, "Ha, you long-living one!" which signified, "You have been fine to us; we have liked it here."

Ceremony with the chiefs is of course more involved, but even with them one may soon relax into the desert familiarity of good-fellowship and easy humor.

We had pleasant company on our ride to Nuri's camp, but not Akhu-Atika's gang of raiders. They had been ordered by Nuri to proceed immediately to Nauaf's camp, to fight against the Shammar in Jauf.

The old men and their women whom we had accompanied from Damascus traveled with us again. I was glad to be alone once more with these courageous, laughing friends. I liked the way they, like all outdoor people, grinned at unpleasantness with a toss of their heads, strangely like that of their brave little mares.

From the black brow of a hill we rode down between grey boulders surrounding an island of purple pasture. The blue mare pricked up her ears and kicked her heels in merriment. The old man released her lead rope from his camel saddle, and the little lady pranced away, greedily burying her nose in the wild flowers. Ghazal and Marzuki's stallion, also scenting the special herbage, a favorite of all desert horses, joined in the feast.

At the same moment the supercilious Alia abandoned her solemn meditations. She lowered her neck, sniffed the plants, and mumbled to the herd with deep groans, bemoaning the ravenous appetite of Ghazal and the other horses. Ignoring the riders on their backs, who were laughing and talking to each other, the herd quickly joined her and scooped up the purple delicacies. Back and forth, to the left and right, like vacuum cleaners, their hairy lips swished over the ground as they shaved off every vestige of green. Their long lower lips dripped juice from the sweet thistle fodder.

It was hard to believe that in so short a time the beauty and fragrance of that little purple island were gone. The dreamy, half-closed eyes and heaving sides of Alia betrayed that she had properly cheated Ghazal.

In the southwest we came upon a close-cropped plain dotted with the black tents and fawn-colored camels of the supreme chief of the Ruala. Armed men on nimble mares galloped toward us to guide us to the tent of the old slave Hamar, where the grey-bearded Prince Nuri sat in council.

Nuri arose and received us ceremoniously, waiting for us at the entrance of the tent with his retainers and his heavily armed bodyguard. I saw a man with prominent features and the eyes of an eagle. He looked like an old patriarch. With an indomitable personality marking him as a leader of men, he instantly commanded my respect. His face resembled a map of his country, lined with wrinkles like dry river beds, pitted with smallpox scars like dry rain pools of the desert. When he spoke, his eyes lighted up in kindly fashion, and his smile was wonderfully gentle. It was difficult to reconcile this kindly old patriarch with the fierce Bedouin fighter that he was, the killer of two of his own brothers and scores of other men in battle.

Nuri motioned us to camel-saddle seats facing the coffee hearth. Nuri settled himself upon his own camel saddle next to the hearth. Its extra layer of rugs and soft cushions and skins marked it as the seat of the chieftain. His relatives, other famous chiefs of the Ruala, and his favorite slaves ranged themselves in successive circles, extending far outside the tent.

Nuri reached out his hand to the coffee cook, who gave him a small cup of the thick liquid. Nuri poured it on the ground in memory of the first Bedouin who had served this stimulating beverage to his guests. Again the cook poured out the customary measure, less than two teaspoonfuls, and Nuri offered the cup to me. I hesitated a moment, waiting for the drink to cool.

"Revive thyself," he said.

These were his first words and his welcome. Next Marzuki was served, and Nuri would not taste of his own cup until all his guests had partaken.

This is the communion of the desert brotherhood, a sacred ceremony emphasizing good will and honor among men.

A boy of about nine years rushed into the mejlis (council of chiefs) and leaned against the old man. While the talk proceeded, Nuri's fingers almost absent-mindedly caressed the head of the child, Fuaz by name, the youngest son of Nauaf.

I felt that however caressing the hand of the old man, it

was never very far away from the silver hilt of his khanjar, or curved dagger.

The meeting continued until long after midnight. Nuri's touches of humor enlivened every conversation, and with so many "heroes and horse thieves" present, as Nuri described the assembly, the council was especially animated.

Marzuki surpassed himself in talkativeness, describing our journey in rich detail and the adventures that had befallen us since we had met in Sheykh Ammer's tent in Egypt.

Nuri, of course, knew Sheykh Ammer, for one of his sons was married to Sheykh Ammer's sister. And Rashayd, whom we had met in Amrieh with his dapple-grey mare Wudiyeh, had been fighting with Nauaf against the Shammar in Jauf.

"Ha wallah—by God!" Nuri said to Marzuki, "was it by your design that Wudiyeh conceived her foal?"

Marzuki looked at me and I looked at Marzuki. We were too surprised to speak.

Nuri shook a playful finger at Marzuki and queried, "Did the generous idea dwell in thy heart to free Rashayd's virgin mare and let her be el-Kaha—in foal—to this Kedish—outcast—stallion of Egypt?"

Gazhal had never been thus insulted!

Marzuki cleared his throat, spat into the fire, and said, almost choking, "By the dispensation of God, may my countenance be blackened, and thy days, O Nuri, be lenghtened, if Rashayd released such a thought upon thee. God pity him!"

Nuri laughed heartily. "And may Rashayd's heart be torn from him and cast to his own dogs if he hath indulged in a lie."

Marzuki jumped to his feet, shouting, "Indeed, Alillah— God is my witness, it was ordained by the Dispenser of Life that this gallant horse and his mistress were to be mated. It was not our design. And Ghazal, God give him strength, is not a Kedish but of the company of the Asilat—noble-born —and el-Quwadi—the led ones. He is of the fast and enduring runners, the Drinkers of the Wind, bestowed upon us by our forefather Ishmael."

Nuri only smiled. These jokes and Marzuki's excitement were to his liking. "Then rejoice that thou hast brought the Drinker of the Wind back into the pastures of his birth. Wilt thou lead him to me?" he said.

I went to fetch Ghazal.

The night was dark, and two slaves accompanied me. We found my horse being guarded by men of the tribe—a courtesy to their guest. They unshackled Ghazal, and I led him back to the tent.

In my absence Marzuki must have told the story of Ghazal in Tripoli and also of how he had killed Aktu-Atika, for when I approached with my horse, Nuri and his council of men rose to show their respect for Ghazal. Bedouins often pay such a tribute to a war mare, but as they never ride stallions on their raids, this was a unique event.

"Aziz, we are honored to call thee our friend," Nuri said to me with dignity, "but thy horse is nearer to us—he is our *kinsman.*"

The old chief lifted his shepherd coat from his shoulders to drop it before Ghazal.

"Shair," he said to a slave. The slave hurried off to another tent and returned with a wooden bowl filled with barley and a clump of dried dates.

Nuri poured the barley upon the shepherd coat, and began to feed the dates to my horse. "Thou black-skinned antelope," he said to Ghazal, "thou large-eyed one!" And he stroked and patted him.

While Ghazal was still munching the dates, dropping the stones from his lips, Nuri picked up one of the pits and handing it to his young grandson, Fuaz, asked him to keep the stone as a token.

"It is well to remember the horse of thy youth; a hero who takes our shadows away."

Nuri seated himself, and a smile touched his eyes as he watched Ghazal eat the barley from the silver-embroidered shepherd coat.

That night, before we slept, Nuri picked up the cloak from which Ghazal had eaten his first supper in the great chief's tent and with his own hands placed it upon my shoulders before the many witnesses. The toga was not simply a gift but a symbolic token that henceforth I stood under Nuri's personal protection in the desert.

These Ruala under Nuri lived by a spiritual code of honor and ancient traditions; they were happy with the merest necessities of life at its simplest. Their forbidding appearance, at first so like the desert, was but a cloak. They were gentle and courteous, and they had made room in their hearts for friendship with a stranger like me.

Stirred by their friendship and by their feeling for their animals, more than ever the search for the perfect horse returned to my mind. I realized that the purchase of mares was not to be an easy task. The gradual desiccation of inner Arabia and the consequent years of prolonged drought were having their tragic effect upon horse breeding, and the mortality among horses in the desert was great. And yet Nuri generously begged me to roam as I pleased with Marzuki among the clans, to see all the horses and meet their owners.

*Grecian
Sculpture
from the
Frieze of
the Parthenon*

*A Young Arabian
Stallion, Showing
the Characteristics
of the Ancient
Thessalian Horse*

Ruala Mounted for Action,
and *(below) the "Led-One"*
in the Desert

The She-Camel, Friend and Constant Companion of the War Mare

Bedouin of the Nufud
"Only the night and my mare know me."

She-Camel with Fawn-Colored Foals

The Ruala Breaking Camp for the Long Migration

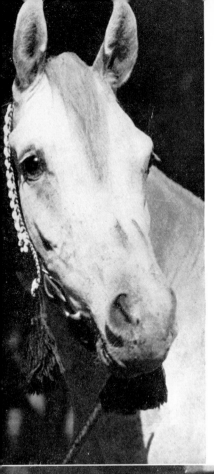

Three Drinkers
of the Wind

Ruala with Crescent-Rigged Camels,
and (below) Slaves Loading Tents

Perfect Arabian—
The Object
of
My Quest

Pastures were improving with fresh showers. Often a flurry of rain overtook us on our rides between the tents of the tribe. Perhaps a clear rain pool gleamed before us then in a hollow, and on tipping a rise we would sight another camp of Ruala and descend upon them to make new friends.

Although I had been with the Ruala three weeks, I had not yet bought any of their horses. Not one of the animals I had seen compared to those of the Parthenon frieze. None had the crescent neck, the rounded lines, the clean head, the fine features and molding of the ancient horses. These mares of the Ruala looked plain and rough, with scars of old wounds from lances and branding irons. They were undernourished and undersized; their legs and hoofs, abused; and their coats of shaggy hair, coarse and unkempt. One could see, however, that in spite of their rough exterior, these animals were well proportioned, and they were possessed of great endurance. But as for beauty, these Bedouin horses were far removed, in comparison, from the horses of old Greece.

Marzuki felt very disappointed because I could not see quality in any of these small, emaciated Bedouin horses. But he would not influence me to make a hasty purchase. Very calmly he told me that I would learn more by observation and that because of my youth I would need much experience.

4

AFTER WE HAD returned to Nuri's camp, a party of Ruala fighters rode to the chief's tent with Nauaf at their head. Among Nauaf's men was my friend Rashayd ibn Whafa.

As Rashayd made his camel couch before Nuri's tent, I pulled the halter rope of his mare from the camel saddle and led Wudiyeh—for of course it was she—behind the tent to hobble her feet. I had not yet betrayed my identity nor had Rashayd looked at me as he followed Nauaf to greet Nuri.

I fetched a bowl of camel's milk for the mare and another vessel of the sweet beverage for Ghazal, who was staked far out in the open between two rows of tents. He sniffed at the milk, looking me over with his large, calm eyes.

"Ishrab—drink," I urged him.

Ghazal dipped his lips into the bowl and sipped slowly, but he kept his gaze on me all the while. I thought I found a questioning look in his eyes. Had he discovered the scent of Wudiyeh?

As I walked away with the empty dish, Ghazal gave me a ringing neigh. He strained at the hobbles and kicked against the rope. He paid no heed to my sharp command, but reared on his hindfeet as far as the rope would allow. I rushed back to Ghazal, seized his halter, and slipped the rope from the tent peg to set him free. He calmed at once when I laid my hand upon him. Perfectly at ease and well-mannered now, he allowed me to lead him to Wudiyeh.

There were squeals when the two friends met—the golden chestnut, with the white star on his forehead, and the dapple-grey mare with the long blaze across her face. Wudiyeh's ears pricked forward, her eyes a-shining, and her nostrils flared as she greeted Ghazal. He seemed to be in a fury, shaking his mane and lashing the air with his tail. But it was only pleasure over the unexpected meeting with the little mare of whom he was so fond.

He squealed as I put my arm around his neck and laid my other hand upon Wudiyeh. With a hard thud Ghazal tossed his muzzle into my cheek as if in warning. And indeed, Nuri and his guests had left the tent and walked right into our path. One of the robed Bedouins came up to me and pulled a gun. It was Rashayd, the old tough. He lifted his arm to point the gun at me, but behind him everyone laughed, a great roar of laughter like the wind—and I laughed, too, and tried to step up to Rashayd, but he cried, "Stay thou—surrender!"

"Dakhilak—before thy countenance!" I said, and took off my head veil and the cord and held them in my hand as a sign of complete surrender.

"Remove thy 'aba!" he commanded.

I dropped Nuri's coat from my shoulders.

Rashayd turned to Nuri, saying, "Is this the man known among all thy people as the-one-who-rides-under-Nuri's cloak?" And when Nuri nodded, Rashayd asked, "May I deal with him as I wish?"

"Thou mayest!" cried Nuri, and everyone shouted with laughter again.

In the next moment Rashayd had his arms around me, but he still held the gun. I took it from him and put it back in its holster.

"Our life is the weft of a loom," Marzuki the poet said, "and each day, like a thread dropped by the breath of God. Thus we have accepted the will of our Creator and retained the virtues of our brotherhood."

"It bids fair to be a real companionship," Rashayd said laughingly, and reminded us that we had sworn friendship by the life which once had been within the withered stalk.

Nuri's son Nauaf, whom I met in these eventful days, did not impress me. He lacked the personality of the supreme sheykh—the gift to organize and unite his own section of the tribe and his warriors under a dominant will. He was shy and silent, as if always occupied with secret problems, and was most at ease in a comfortable corner of the tent with one or two trusted friends near him. Though a true Bedouin, he had by temperament the longing for a peaceful place in which to rule. This place was Jauf.

From the days of old the Ruala had peacefully traded with Jauf, an oasis at the southeastern end of the wide, fertile depression of the Wadi Sirhan. During the last two years the Ibn Rashids, the ruling princes of the Shammar tribes, hereditary enemies of the Ruala, had subjugated Jauf and the greater part of inner Arabia; whereupon Jauf became the objective of long and bitter fighting between the two tribes.

Bedouins draw a very distinctive line between a ghazu (raid) and harb (a war expedition). They have an ancient, chivalrous code of raiding which allows them to drive off a number of camels and horses from their enemies—without shedding blood, if possible, not only out of regard for the life of their foes, but because they fear the blood feud of avengers. For that reason, and also out of regard for the safety of their women and children, Bedouins never fight near their camps.

But the princes of the Shammar tribes, in contrast to those of the Ruala, carried war and destruction into the tents of the Ruala, causing wanton murder among the innocent. If it had not been for Nuri's leniency, extensive reprisals would have been taken against the Shammar, but Nuri allowed his son to muster armed men only against the Shammar in Jauf. The migrating desert clans of the Shammar remained unmolested.

Made stubborn by the resistance of Jauf, Nauaf longed more than ever to assemble a force sufficient to defeat the Rashids and their Shammar tribes.

Like his father, Nauaf was in constant fear of his life and found it advisable to have his neighborhood guarded by warriors. I saw him go hungry for five days, whether in self-denial or in fear of poisoning, I cannot say, though during that interval he played the lavish host to hundreds of guests. His son, Fuaz, not older than nine, was forbidden to touch anything but camel's milk during a time of fasting. He was taught while young to endure hunger courageously, to show hardihood and courtesy in every situation. Though the little boy could not read or write, when called upon to help an old woman with her load of waterskins or desert brush, he would almost outdo any servant of his father's house. He gathered desert seeds and truffles, did the churning of butter or the setting up of tents. He rode the camels to pasture with herdsmen, looked after his father's mares and his own, helped to train falcons and gazelle hounds. He was a good marksman, too, shooting with double-barreled shotguns, as well as army rifles.

Though Fuaz' legs were as yet rather short to grip the flanks of a mare and his arms too weak to balance a carbine for any length of time, yet the hard life of the desert had given this young boy the reputation of being an adroit rider.

His blind mother, Misha'il, proudly told me that it had been an omen of good for the future that old Nuri had laid the halter of his war mare and a silver khanjar in the child's cradle at birth, for it was the same curved dagger with which Nuri had killed in single combat the chieftain of the Muntifiq.

Fuaz liked to practice with the mirdaha, or slingshot, the ancient desert weapon with which with a single pebble David felled Goliath. The Bedouins can slay a man in this fashion at sixty feet; on horseback they take better aim with a sling-shot than with a gun.

One afternoon in Nauaf's camp young Fuaz and a company of boys and young slaves were practicing with their slings. They shot flat pebbles with astounding accuracy at the foot-high wooden pegs of a tent some thirty paces distant. Unseen by them, I suddenly stepped out from behind Nauaf's tent. A stone, which had hit its target close to me, rebounded from the smooth wood and struck me on the forehead, between the eyes.

For a moment I was stunned. My first thought was that I had been struck by a bullet.

Gasping, and with frightened face, Fuaz ran up to me. At once he saw the wound on my forehead and the few drops of blood on my fingers, which I had in my confusion pressed to my head. I urged him and the other children crowding around us to forget the trivial accident and go on with their play.

They would not listen, but mentioned, again and again, the blood. Laughingly I took Fuaz in my arms and told him once more that it was no great matter.

A look of anger crossed his face, as if he were offended. He wriggled free to stand still before me. Then he tore his aghal and kaffiyeh—the cord and kerchief—from his head, letting the six fine braids fall over his shoulders. With tears welling from defiant eyes, he cried, "Ana Dakhilak—before the face of God I surrender myself unto thee. Tell me the price of thy blood."

His voice was not regretful nor did it suggest any wish to be forgiven. The young prince was defiant because he thought I had ridiculed his offer.

My heart went out to the wild little creature. He had the blood of his father's guest on his conscience, and he thought only of the satisfaction due to me. He was anxious to settle the blood price with me before the news reached the ears of his father and the council of men.

How much blood was shed—in this case, only a few drops —did not matter; the one thing of account was the unwritten Bedouin law which secures to the stranger inviolability, even in the tent of the humblest nomad. The blood price of a guest, I learned, was reckoned twice as high as that of a man killed in fight—fifty camels and four mares.

I wanted to smile when I thought of the high value set on a few drops of my blood. But I composed my face to solemnity and, calling the other boys as witnesses, said to Fuaz, "This happened according to the will of God. I know only one price—thy friendship."

Fuaz stared at me wide-eyed. He could not believe that a stranger should invoke the ancient custom of his forefathers.

I did not realize at that instant the great price I was demanding.

Suddenly he flung away the fateful sling and advanced to me with outstretched arms, clasping my neck with childish affection as I bent down to him. I held him close and kissed him on both cheeks. With his finger he lightly dabbed the scratch on my forehead, then rubbed four drops of blood on his own forehead between his black brows—the age-old Bedouin Nured-Dam, the rite of blood.

In this unusual fashion I became the blood brother of Amir Fuaz. And to this child I owed the fact that I was privileged to live with the Ruala as one of them, that I was able to visit them many times over a period of twenty-six years, and that sixteen summers later I was adopted into the tribe as a Rueyli chieftain to help them in their war against the nine tribes.

Long years after this incident of the slingshot, Fuaz said to me, "Now do I understand for the first time the words I learned from my mu'allim: 'Thou who followest with thine eyes the flight of a bird or the course of the pebble flung from thy hand, what knowest thou of God's purposes?' "

The time was at hand for a final demonstration against the Shammar at Jauf. The Ruala planned, therefore, to make a combined show of power. They would carry with them the Ark of Ishmael, the tabernacle of the tribes, the altar before which Bedouins for centuries have made their votive offerings. There is only one such markab—ship or ark—in all Arabia. For generations it has moved from tribe to tribe, as one conquered the other. The Ruala have held it for nearly one hundred and fifty years, and it has become the symbol of their unity and their emblem of war—their great tribal banner. In grave and decisive conflicts this ancient and hallowed standard, the Ruala told me, had been moved by the Spirit of Allah to reveal to them when and where to face the enemy and join in battle.

A large framework made of light desert acacia wood, the Ark was adorned with hundreds of small tufts of black ostrich feathers. It was kept in Nuri's tent. Now it would be borne on the back of a camel as the Ruala made their ceremonial expedition to Jauf. Massed together in an immense swarm extending over fifteen miles in width, they came surging across the desert, with all their pack animals, horses, and dogs following.

For nine hours we rode and then camped for the night. In the morning we mounted again, and the strange horde moved on. We must have proceeded forty-five miles from Nuri's camp before we came into sight of Jauf. The depression around Jauf, as far as the eye could see, began to fill with the heaving mass of our camels. The air vibrated with the drone of voices—men's and beasts'—and the din of movement. On both sides guns were fired, and the shouting and shooting lasted for hours as we approached closer to the oasis.

Although Nuri could easily have taken Jauf in a serious attack, he considered the losses that would be inflicted upon both sides and decided upon a barbaric though rather harmless demonstration of his armed force. This display was merely designed to point out to the settlers of Jauf the divine and ancient mission of the Ruala in Desert-Arabia, and to overawe the unbelievers and the superstitious among them.

In the morning the Ruala rode from appointed stations in the valley with their sacred Ark and ascended from the plains to the hills opposite Jauf.

"There is no God like the God of Nuri," they shouted,

"Who advances to our aid on camels and dissolves our foes concealed in Jauf."

The firing of rifles had ceased on both sides. The vanguard of the Ruala approached the walled oasis with measured strides. After the Ruala had circled Jauf a second time, Nauaf rode forth boldly to the mud walls of the oasis and laid his javelin down at the gate of the village as a pledge of peace. The enemies cheered, but none surrendered or gave a sign to open the gates.

Night fell and the Ruala withdrew. Immense fires were built, illuminating the whole countryside. A camel was sacrificed before the Ark as a burnt offering, and the bones of the animal were thrown into the embers of our hearth. Nuri and his great host departed toward the desert as the moon rose in the valley of Sirhan.

With songs of love and of the glory of their horses and camels on their lips, the Ruala returned to their old pasture grounds. They had only intimidated their enemy, but nevertheless they were elated by the glory of the picture they had seen of their own migrating nation. The expedition had realized the Ruala to themselves.

5

THE ASSEMBLY of the tribes and their demonstration against Jauf had presented to me an unusual opportunity to examine the horses of each clan, but all I saw was the same emaciated, undersized, rough type of war mares. Halfheartedly I looked at every strange horse, still hoping; but I began to admit to myself that I was defeated, that my childhood dream of finding a horse, noble like those of the ancients, had been in vain. Marzuki was already talking about our return to Damascus when an unforeseen disaster upset all our plans.

It happened during our visit in Rashayd's camp, as we were taking our repast with him. Seizing his binoculars, he gazed for a long time at the horizon. Suddenly, without a word to us, Rashayd rushed to the entrance of our tent, and began to signal some nearby women with the long sleeves of his garment. By gesture the women conveyed the message that all horses and camels must be brought in. In a flash the whole camp came to life. Young boys, girls, and women unhobbled the mares and rode out to the nearest hills to call the armed guards and herdsmen in the pastures.

I was amazed at the way in which, by this almost unnoticeable method of signals, messages traveled within a few moments a distance that it would have taken an hour or more to carry on horseback.

The cause of all this excitement was a scouting party of Nauaf's approaching the camp. Rashayd mounted his mare and galloped out to meet them. They and their horses were in an utterly exhausted condition. One mare was blood-spattered from her halter to her girth. These few men and their horses were the remnants of one of the scouting parties. Originally twenty-three men, they had been reconnoitering in the Hamad, east of our camp, and there a large group of Iban Rashid's Shammar Bedouins had ambushed and wantonly killed nineteen of them.

Within the hour Rashayd had assembled over two hundred and fifty race camels and almost a hundred mares. The riders waited in front of our tent with carbines in hand, cartridge belts across their shoulders and daggers in their sashes. Lightly they swung into their saddles, and Rashayd himself took command.

For a long time I had desired to ride on a raid with the Ruala, but Marzuki always warned me of the hardships and dangers. Now with Rashayd's and Mnahi's persuasive powers aiding my case, Marzuki consented to my going on this foray against the Shammar.

Our camel troop was lightly provisioned except for water. Rashayd's plan was to overtake the Shammar as quickly as we could by riding our camels and leading the horses. Only for the final attack upon the enemy would our mares be mounted.

To my surprise, Rashayd tied Wudiyeh to his race camel and asked me to take Ghazal along, though the Bedouins seldom used stallions on a raid. It seemed to me that all senti-ment had suddenly gone out of Rashayd, as the light of a candle is blown out by wind. I asked if Wudiyeh might not remain behind because she was in foal. Rashayd shook his head, answering roughly that she must take her chances with the others. For Ghazal's and Wudiyeh's sake I was glad that both horses were to stay together.

Rashayd expected that we would be gone a week or two at the most. But even a seasoned raider like Rashayd, commander of the camel saddles, could err. Leaving in such extreme haste, my farewell to Marzuki was very brief. "Thy journey will be an arduous one," Marzuki said. He lifted his arm to shade his eyes and looked to the east, over miles of barren desert, colored and enriched by ever-changing lights and shadows. "This journey will free thy spirit," he continued. "Take care of the fawn of the desert." He laid his hand on Ghazal and kissed him. Then he wandered over to Wudiyeh, and threw one fold of his shepherd's coat over his shoulder and at the same time over the head of Wudiyeh, as a lover would do taking farewell of his bride. "The Bedouins, and all whom the wind claws," I heard him say in his gentle voice to Wudiyeh. She watched him softly with a quiet wisdom, and Marzuki repeated, "The Bedouins, and all upon whom the wind blows."

These words are mystic, derived from an ancient proverb of the desert. The meaning of the words is manifold. They may apply to the living or to the dead, and the wind may be the spirit and the breath of God.

"Let us go now," Marzuki said to me, "and promise that we shall not feel very old and very far from each other."

Such words were again of his spiritual apprehension of the truth that we were not to worry about time or distance or events, but entrust our souls completely to the hands of God.

I promised him that his kindly words of advice and his spirit of gaiety would come to me with every desert breeze. I followed him with my eyes as we rode away. In his flowing shepherd coat he looked the true Ishmaelite. Long hair plaited in dark love locks framed his oval face. I could see him still gazing after me with his dark eyes. I lost sight of him finally when we disappeared beyond a rise in the ground, but his strength, the warmth of his great soul, I did not lose. It went out with me on the great raid against the Shammar. . . .

Our troop rode after dark until we reached a long chain of small rain pools. Here an intense surprise came to us. The men, rearranging their riding gear and waterskins, discovered in one of the saddlebags the princely son of their master, nine year old Fuaz, curled up and sound asleep.

Not by the slightest noise had he betrayed to us during the long hard ride that we were carrying a stowaway. Indeed, he had long ago become used to such travel. In the days when he had been too small to ride, the slaves had put him with his brothers into the camel saddlebags. He confessed now that he had decided not to miss a raid against the hated Shammar and to prove his valor as a prince of the Ruala should.

Rashayd wanted the boy taken home by a camel rider, but Fuaz pleaded so earnestly that the heart of the freebooter was softened. I gave Rashayd a solemn promise to look after the child as if he were my own son. Rashayd at once dispatched a man on a fast dhalul to Misha'il, the blind mother of Fuaz, to let her know that her boy was with us.

When no one else was near enough to overhear us, the young prince said to me, "Wallah—by God—there is no need for you to protect me, but when an emergency arises, we shall defend each other."

It seemed we were blood brothers in fact as well as in ceremony, the young prince of the desert and the stranger from abroad.

110

Fuaz led me over to a camel; he reached deep into the bag, searching anxiously. "I cannot find him, Aziz. Wilt thou help me?"

I could find nothing in the saddlebag. I asked him what he had lost.

"My little dog," he cried, and I noticed that his eyes were bright with tears. He told me that he had put the dog into a camel bag before he himself slipped into another.

It was surprising to me that he could remember, among so many camels, the particular one he had selected. But he was a Bedouin.

To Mnahi, the chief of the slaves and the owner of the camel, Fuaz said, "Thou brutal dib—wolf—on whom there is no room for grace, thou hast contrived the death of my hero and hast thrown the defender of my mother's house into the wilderness, a prey to vultures."

Then, Bedouin fashion, he exalted the virtues of the dog, a little puppy not more than a fortnight old. (The "defender of his mother's house," which could have done no more than chase a flea from its tail!)

Mnahi enlightened Fuaz, saying that he had heard the noise of the puppy in his camel saddlebag just before leaving the home camp and had thrown him out. He suspected that someone had intended an insult by sending an "unclean" animal along.

"Shame!" Fuaz cried. "May God rob thee of thy strength and water thy face with tears because thou hast deprived me of my companion."

At sunup, beyond the dry bed of a wadi, we discovered the first tracks of the enemy. According to Rashayd and our scouts, the Shammar were at least twice as strong as we, all

111

heading southeast, as was evident from the camel droppings. We found, too, the cold ashes of their many campfires.

All day we rode, our horses tossing their heads and blowing hard through dust-filled nostrils. Late in the afternoon, still following the tracks of the Shammar, we came upon another wadi. Here had been the scene of a battle, and the sight that greeted us was gruesome. Hyenas and wolves helped vultures to tear bodies apart and carry them all over the river bed. The stench was such that our horses refused to approach. We had to leave the terrified animals behind as we made our grisly search. Vultures, many too heavy and overfed to soar away, flapped but a few paces from us and could easily have been slain. Nor were the eagles so wary as usual as they hovered upon lazy wings above the cruel feast.

Fuaz felt great pity for the dead mares of the Ruala, which he recognized by their brands. With his camel wand he beckoned to me as he stood beside a bay mare, or what was left of her blood-dyed carcass. "This is Ibn Sumran's war mare," he told me tearfully, "the one that the old Frayje used to lend me to ride on the chase. Now she is clothed in the robe of death."

And Rashayd's voice cried above all others, "Oh, could ye but extinguish the flame of this bitter memory with the edge of your swords."

With compassionate eyes Fuaz looked upon the slaughter-ground made by the Shammar. He swore to Rashayd that we would take vengeance on our enemies.

I could understand then how in each generation the age-long feeling of enmity against the "black princes" of Hayil, the Ibn Rashids and their Shammar, was aroused in the heart of the Ruala youth.

We sat in subdued council that night, some miles away

112

from the scene of battle. Again and again the young prince urged Rashayd to lead us at once in pursuit of the Shammar. The boy did not realize how scanty were our supplies. Our only advantage over the Shammar was our equipment of modern Mauser guns. To pursue the enemy farther into Arabia would mean a great sacrifice of life, for the Shammar might cross the entire desert, almost four hundred miles more, and reach their brother tribes in Iraq. But the hearts of our men, inflamed by that scene of death near us, prevailed upon Rashayd not to turn back to the home camps, but to attempt to waylay the Shammar.

I had not imagined that life in Arabia could be so hideous. My vision of the romance of this spacious desert was blotted out; its gentle, fine people—like Nuri and Marzuki, my old companions—were transformed. These children of good humor and neighborly love had suddenly chilled into incredibly revengeful warriors with only one thought in their minds —to inflict cruel retribution upon their enemies.

Not one of the raiders in our party wanted to turn back. Rashayd was at loss to persuade even one man, as a personal sacrifice, to return the young prince to the Ruala camp.

I had no desire to continue on the raid. It was obviously a ride into the jaws of Hades, not only because of the scorching heat but also the danger of a cruel encounter with the most formidable fighters in Arabia.

But Fuaz would not return to camp; he was elated, and felt that this was the opportunity of his life. And had I not been appointed his protector? So it was not an exultant spirit of adventure or heroism, but the need to save my face that decided me to proceed with Rashayd and his raiders.

Tragedy went with us in everything on that vengeance ride. Out in the sun-stricken land slumbering mirages vanished and reappeared, taunting us. By noon the earth was a shimmering furnace, but our camels plodded forward with easy strides, dragging our horses.

We followed the tracks of the enemy. It was fourteen hours before our scouts, mounted on the sturdiest camels, returned and called a halt. One of them urged us on to ride another hour, reciting, "Forward! Bullets do not kill. The swift runner, under whose feet sparks fly, springs into the thick dust and carries thee courageously into the midst of the fight. Forward!"

We went forward, but with aching limbs and parched throats, and stomachs rumbling with hunger. The scouts promised a good camping place, and they kept their word. In its protection we dared to build a fire that could not be seen from a higher spot.

It was night, and it was cool. We watered and fed our horses, ate hard camel cheese, dates, and liquid butter, and Rashayd let us sleep until after midnight. Then out again into the dark and trackless waste . . . until the scouts proudly pointed out the imprints of the Shammar. If our horses could stand the hardship, we might overtake the enemy with another two days' strenuous riding.

Toward the evening of the first day we sighted on the horizon a large drove of camels in a line too broad to belong to a raiding party. The riders proved to be of the Amarat tribe, of the ruling clan of Ibn Hadhdhal.

Though the Amarat and the Ruala often raided each other, both tribes belonged to the great nomad nation of the Anaza and both held the Shammar to be their bitter enemies. The Amarat killed a number of their young camels for a joint feast, and provided for our horses every drop of camel milk from their huge flock, even depriving the suckling foals of milk that night—a generous gift which proved to be the saving of our horses. At parting next morning the Amarat presented us with several skins of liquid sheep butter, and still more milk from their camels.

With new strength our horses followed in the wake of the camels. All that day we crossed a plain, until finally, toward afternoon, we reached the uprising center of Kirban. Would this be the land of death, my companions wondered? Would our graves be here?

The day was oppressive, doubly so because we sensed the approach of a sandstorm. Gradually we rode into the teeth of it, fighting it from noon on. We were desperate, for the storm spoiled the tracks of the enemy. The wind ceased almost entirely that night. But next morning it came upon us more wildly than ever.

My burning tongue clove to the roof of my mouth; my ears tingled; my eyes were inflamed and my lips chapped and bled. The effort to hold with both hands to the saddle horse weakened me so that I was bathed in sweat. I could see only the two nearest mares and Ghazal, tied to Alia, and six other dhaluls.

Unexpectedly Rashayd appeared at our side, bleeding from a wound under his right eye. "The occasion for strife hath arisen," he cried to me. "Take thy rifle, Aziz, and keep thou an eye on our prince."

I jerked the Mauser out of the holster and slung the two heavy cartridge belts over my shoulder. With new determination I drew the headgear tighter around my head and took a mouthful of it between my teeth. The purgatory of the sandstorm was forgotten. A more cruel enemy had appeared on our stage. The Shammar had run into the left wing of camelry and were firing away when Rashayd and I rode with our cavalry to the rescue. The enemy fled.

At sunset the Shammar attacked us, but they were in the open, exposed to the fire of our guns and paid heavily. Our sentries, reconnoitering all night, returned several times to report that the Shammar were retreating in the direction of wells in Wudi Khada. This could only mean that they had abandoned us to secure water for their mares. There had been sufficient moisture in the scant pasture for camels, but not for horses, and apparently we were not the only ones whose water supply had begun to get dangerously low.

At sunrise Rashayd ordered us to advance to a basin a short distance to the southeast and to occupy some ancient water-holes. Following cautiously behind our scouts, we reached the first pit, but our hope of finding water there was blasted. A ride of ten miles brought us to Haziran, but there the wells were also dry.

In desperation, Rashayd ordered fourteen of our extra camels killed. The paunches and entrails of these camels supplied enough liquid to fill eleven skins of water. Strained through shepherd coats, and mixed with two gallons of milk, drawn from some mother camels, it became sufficiently palatable to our mares. Ghazal also drank the strange beverage.

After this we dared to ride on. Our scouts reported that the Shammar were changing their position again, heading for the well of Burdan, a watering place very close to the cultivated land of Mesopotamia. We rode far into the night; towards morning, the happy message went about that we had already outdistanced the Shammar by many miles.

116

6

Rashayd began to separate our best horses from the dhaluls. He planned to lure the Shammar into an ambush. We left our protected place towards noon and scouted carefully about for more than an hour, when very suddenly we plunged right into the thick of an overwhelming force of mounted Shammar. We turned at once, but our enemies were so close that many jumped off their camels and horses and began firing at us from the ground.

By some strange accident a bullet tore off the rope of Ghazal's headstall in my hand. Only a small piece, less than a foot long, remained, and I had to guide the horse with my legs and by word of mouth.

I felt Ghazal quiver under me with the effort for greater speed. Flecks of foam gathered on his muzzle, and beads of sweat trembled on his coat as he fought his way uphill, fetlock deep in sand. A pungent odor rose from him, the scent of the fighting stallion. The pursuers were gaining on us. Through the wave of another dune Ghazal lunged forward. . . . Then, a sudden false step, and we went down.

I was thrown unhurt, ahead of Ghazal, while our horsemen thundered by. I scrambled to my feet, helped Ghazal to rise, and mounted him again. His first steps were unsteady but soon he gathered speed and drove forward powerfully once more, faster and faster, like a gazelle fleeing from the hunters toward a flock of her own kin. We entered a gravel plain. Swifter and longer grew Ghazal's stride, thundering along on sure hoofs—turning the dry grass beneath to dust.

Completely unaware, the Shammar rode directly into the gunfire of our men, and realizing that any resistance would be useless, they surrendered, one after another. Eagerly I scanned the horses of the enemy as they were led away by our men, hoping to find a perfect specimen, but not one of their animals was finer than those of the Ruala.

But soon the alarm cries of our men told us that the full force of the Shammar had unexpectedly begun their attack upon us. Rashayd moved quietly along the lines giving orders as our left wing began firing. The enemy was swarming about, and it was not long before fifty or more of the most daring riders had passed alive through our fire to reach the wadi on the opposite bank. Sliding off their dhaluls, they took sheltered positions from which they sniped away at our men.

At once Rashayd called our horsemen together, and with at least half their number we dashed along the ravine to a spot high above the invading Shammar, riding through their firing line, up to the rising ground.

A bullet struck my shoulder and knocked me from Ghazal's back to the ground, spraining my leg in the tumble. But in his wild dash Ghazal had already carried me safely out of reach of the enemy. I lay helpless for quite awhile, unable to move. At first I felt pain only slightly, but soon with a burning intensity under my right shoulder blade.

Ghazal stood patiently at my side waiting for me to rise. "U'a, u'a, u'a," I called to him. His flanks quivered and a loud squeal rent the air. He was frightened. He had smelled

118

the blood of my wound. His head sought the ground, and I felt the caress of his nostrils and the play of his warm breath. I stroked his forehead. Whimpering, he backed away from me, but my groping hand followed, and held him on the halter rope.

"Na'm—lie down," I commanded. "Na'm, na'm," I repeated.

He turned around obediently and lay down. With painful effort I pulled myself across his withers and ordered him to rise, while I clung firmly to his mane to keep from sliding off. My left hand was braced on the upper part of his near foreleg. Restrained by my voice, he ventured forward very slowly into a walk.

We had covered half the distance to the edge of the plateau when Ghazal took a sudden step aside and snorted with fright. Until now all my thoughts had been concentrated upon keeping my balance. I had paid no attention to what was happening around me. But on approaching this higher point of the slope, Grazal and I had again come into full view of the enemy below. Bullets whirred into the soil before us; others glanced away with a faint metallic twang.

"Irkud—run!" I cried to Ghazal, and with my hands I urged him forward.

Of a sudden Ghazal stumbled and gave a queer cry of pain.

I knew that he had been wounded. For the second time he faltered and bounded again. Thrusting himself forward, he began to run.

Then I lost my balance and slipped over his back to the earth. My hands broke the force of my fall, and I saw men run toward me. I was picked up and carried to a shelter on the heights above.

By the greatest luck Ghazal and I had escaped the slaughter, though both of us had been badly injured.

Fuaz impatiently waited to come to our plateau after the skirmish was over. With the help of one of the slaves he found me and appeared very much hurt that I had left him in the lurch—as he called it—and ridden off alone without him. Not a word of pity came from his lips as he watched the slaves extract the bullet from my shoulder.

I inquired about Rashayd and Ghazal and Wudiyeh.

"Wudiyeh," one of the slaves said, "is dying, and Ghazal is so badly injured that he will not rise again."

I begged Mnahi and another slave to carry me to Ghazal. He was resting under a clump of bushes at the rim of the wadi. To our great relief, we found him standing on his feet although he favored his near foreleg and could not use it. A bullet had left a deep injury about a hand-wide above his forearm. Mnahi looked at it and thought it would heal naturally if the nerve of the leg could be saved. He prepared a splint and tied up the injured leg in such fashion that it would not have to rest on its hoof.

Ghazal watched us quietly while Mnahi treated him. I stroked his lovelock and straightened his mane. I laid my hand upon his shoulder until I felt his muscles relax and become supple again. The nervous tension was over. He nudged my side, and his weak little voice had a questioning sound.

When Mnahi had finished, he drew his curved khanjar and cut off the strand of hair from Ghazal's forehead. He dropped the hair into my hand. "Remember this day forever," he said, "and the word of the Hadith: 'Weal is braided in the forelocks of our horses until the day of God.'"

Mnahi took my arm and gently led me over to Wudiyeh.

We found her lying on the ground. The sand around her

120

was damp with blood. From nearby tracks we could see how she had staggered and finally dropped to earth. A clod of earth stuffed into a terrible gash in her ribs had stopped the flow of blood.

With the support of our slaves, I bent down to her and lifted her face to my own. She was in agony and helpless and looked at me with broken eyes. She took hold of my shepherd cloak with her teeth and bit hard; thus she held up her head until her strength failed her and the coat dropped from her teeth.

A bullet would have been merciful and would have saved her further anguish. That, however, was for Rashayd to decide.

We went next to see him and found him surrounded by a group of camel riders. Rashayd had also been injured. His right hand was completely shattered. To make it insensible to pain, a slave tightened his arm with a cord above his wrist, and Mnahi made ready to amputate the mutilated hand.

Half-jokingly, Rashayd scolded me for having followed him on this ride to the plateau, but at the same time he assured me that I would recover quickly from my injury. He warned his men not to climb down to the dry river bed where the dead enemy lay scattered about, for he expected a new attack of the Shammar camel riders from the other side of the wadi.

Anxiously I broke in upon Rashayd's talk, asking him what should be done for Wudiyeh.

He would look after her, he promised me.

Mnahi returned with a baking iron and camel fat. The tallow melted quickly over a blazing fire. Then Mnahi drew his sword, while another man held Rashayd's arm.

All the while, Rashayd was holding his old spy glass in his

uninjured hand. He had just discovered forty camels at the steep sand walls below, and indifferent to his own pain and the imminent operation, asked those around him to capture them.

Mnahi impatiently asked the master if he could proceed to cut his hand off.

Rashayd forced a smile upon his face and said, "Indeed, take my burden away."

With one stroke the gallant leader's hand was severed. Immediately, the slave who supported the arm, plunged the mutilated stump into the boiling fat. This was too much even for Rashayd; he fainted.

During these critical moments the Shammar attacked us again but were easily repulsed by our men from well-prepared defenses. The assault was already over when Rashayd recovered his senses. His first words were for the missing hand. Someone had carelessly thrown it into the sand. He ordered a thorough search for it, and after it was found, asked that it should be tied to his camel saddle.

I had asked to go back to Wudiyeh. She lifted her head from the ground as the slaves and I approached. The poor emaciated animal was almost spent and had broken out in a terrible sweat—her nostrils dripping and the breath flying from her. To relieve the pain, I rubbed her face briskly, and Fuaz helped me to stroke her neck. I asked the child to bring a bowl of milk, but the mare would not touch it though she suffered acutely from thirst. Her eyes were feverish, and the froth upon her lips was turning red with blood. She coughed, then suddenly fell over on her side.

This must be the end, I thought, and I begged Fuaz to run for Rashayd.

Shivers were wracking the pitiable form of the little mare. Her disheveled mane hung shaggy upon the ground. Her coat was lusterless, matted with sweat and blood. Her brown eyes stared at me, her soul frightened by the nearness of death. As the light fled from her eyes, I thought of the foal she bore, the child of her love and of Ghazal. . . .

Wudiyeh lay with closed eyes now. Her even breath was the only proof that she still lived. The beauty of her little body was marred by the dark clod of earth stuffed into her wound.

Rashayd arrived with his slaves and the boy prince.

Wudiyeh opened her eyes and whinnied to her master with bloodstained lips; she made no effort to rise. Rashayd bent down—the mutilated man beside the dying mare. He looked as worn and gaunt as his horse.

"Thou hast carried my life," he said to her.

He touched her lean shanks, felt the wound, and pulled at the clump of earth. He pushed it back quickly and poured fresh sand upon the injury. He was so weak that his slaves had to help him to his feet.

"When the morning sun toucheth the east, if Wudiyeh still liveth, she will remain with us," he said.

I felt as if the twilight around us were already the new dawn. Rashayd had given us hope where there had been no hope at all.

"Ishrabu—drink." Rashayd tried gently to persuade Wudiyeh to take the milk Fuaz had earlier brought her. I held the bowl as Rashayd coaxed her with soft words. This time she sniffed at the bowl and slowly emptied it.

"Wallah," cried Rashayd, and we all spoke encouragingly to Wudiyeh.

123

In the meantime three chiefs of the Shammar had arrived under a flag of truce with a suggestion of terms for an honorable peace. Before witnesses Rashayd and the Shammar formally promised to cease hostilities. Now they drank coffee together—in itself a pledge not to lift a hand against each other.

Peace had been restored. Although no covenant of friendship had been pronounced, there need be no fear of renewed enmity. True Bedouins of the desert respect their unwritten code of honor.

I stayed with Rashayd and Mnahi near Wudiyeh's side all night. Although feverish, she drank milk again. And because Rashayd's heart was sad and burdened with pain, he told me Wudiyeh's story.

"The long-maned one with the swift pace, the destroyer of raiders, was a gift of my father at his death. I kept her in his memory, and bestowed upon her the name of my uncle's daughter—Wudiyeh. There was no blemish in my cousin's beauty, and there is none in my little mare who followed the girl's footprints in our home pastures. A mist covers my eyes when I remember how my beloved walked with such light yet strong strides and with such grace, and, oh, the depth of her eyes."

Could the speaker be that hardened warrior we all knew, the veteran of many a cruel raid?

His thoughts flowed on, as he laid his hand upon the mare's forehead. "Wudiyeh, my shy antelope with the blue hair. How thou hast loved the spear in my hand, and lunged forward with me to smite the enemy. Together, we were never alone and never afraid. Now is thy path sprinkled with the dew of thy blood. Thou art pasturing under the shadow of

124

death. The thunder of thy hoofs hath died, but the echo soundeth in my heart. Undaunted friend, Wudiyeh."

I had wondered why Rashayd was so cruel as to take his mare into this raid. Now I knew that she was all he had, and he could not have faced the raid without her.

For nine days, Wudiyeh's life hung in the balance, and we often despaired of her strength to pull through. On the tenth day, however, when she passed the crisis, there was great rejoicing, and Rashayd said to me, "God has turned her from the snares of death."

And Mnahi exclaimed, "Her eyes have the glance of dawn. She gazes with longing heart to the dwellings of our spacious land. God has looked upon her path, and He alone knows the secret of her days."

The Homecoming of the Horses

AN AGHEYL, a camel trader, whose caravan had come from Baghdad to the well of Burdan to draw water, had loaned us a white canvas tent. There had been a sudden relapse in my condition, and Rashayd and Mnahi insisted that I give my injured back a complete rest. They prepared living quarters for me and the young prince in this tent. Mosquito curtains protected us from flies, which, now that our migratory life had ceased, descended upon us. Mnahi insisted that he massaged Ghazal's leg daily, applied linaments and warm linseed packs, and that Ghazal was feeling better every day.

Early one morning, while I was still bedded on my soft pile of fur skins and rugs, Rashayd, with a grin on his face, entered my tent and asked me if I knew the sound of the feet coming toward us. I listened; the beat of slowly moving hoofs fell upon my ears. Rashayd laid a finger to his lips and walked out.

Coupled with the warning shouts of Mnahi, I heard the loud, silvery neigh of a horse. I rose to have a look through an opening in the canvas and beheld Ghazal fighting Mnahi, trying to get away from him. It looked as if Ghazal would strike, but he only pranced about and pulled the headstall rope from Mnahi's hand. Once free, Ghazal turned his hindquarters toward Mnahi, lifted one foot halfheartedly, and edged Mnahi aside with his hocks.

127

With a loud neigh Ghazal flew toward my tent. I had not time to save myself. The entrance was suddenly darkened as Ghazal dashed into the tent and brought it down upon me. Canvas and broken tent supports covered me. With all my strength I tried to keep the weight of Ghazal's body from my injured back. I felt his muzzle thrust into my face as he snorted and squealed.

"Ghazali," I cried at the top of my lungs, but he continued to poke me, uttering unearthly grunts.

I felt his quivering side. I could hear the thumping of his heart.

"Uskut, uskut—calm yourself!" I shouted, having found my Arabic again. "Warra-warra—stand back!"

At last Ghazal obeyed me and allowed my friends to lead him away and remove me from the ruins of the tent.

"I shall have to move you into a new tent," Rashayd called to me.

"Very well, Rashayd," I said, "but give me one large enough so Ghazal can walk in and out without breaking it down."

Rashayd did more than I asked of him. He bought the biggest tent of the Agheyls, one large enough to hold Ghazal and Wudiyeh, too.

In this fashion our happy household existed for eleven days. Mnahi continued to take care of our horses and look after our strange menage.

Wudiyeh's and Ghazal's injuries were healing rapidly now, and they were out every day for exercising walks. It was touching to see Ghazal's and Wudiyeh's concern for me. For an hour sometimes Wudiyeh would stand at my side, her large eyes shining as she gazed at me.

"Hubini—my beloved," I called.

128

She bent her head to me and her lips twitched over my arm. As my hand went from her neck to her shoulder and down to her side, I felt the ugly scar. She whinnied softly, as if in self-sympathy. Also Ghazal, quieted now, would come to my side and allow me to play with him as I lay on my sheepskin bedding. He liked to swish the hair of his short tail into my hand so that I could grap it; then he would sweep it out of my reach and, with a quick powerful jerk, bring it back to me. This play could go on indefinitely.

He never strayed far from the tent alone. He would come back often, putting his head through the entrance to look at me with soft, curious eyes, as if he wanted to make sure that I was all right or as if he were asking my permission to stay away a while longer.

During these days of convalescence together our friendship deepened, and I was learning the healing quality of time. The shock to body and mind gave way to a measure of peace. Ghazal and Wudiyeh had returned from death and my own life had been spared. Once again I felt eager to pursue my search for the perfect horse.

Rashayd awaited reports of late rains in the Wudiyan and Hamad before he would risk the long journey back to the Ruala camps.

I felt lonesome and, for the first time, in the grip of a mood to give up everything. Baghdad was so near, I could have gone on a boat to Egypt, by way of India and the Rea Sea. A pleasant trip at this time of the year, and I shuddered at the thought of going back to the desert. The terrible experiences of the last few weeks were only too real to me. But Rashayd and Mnahi, intercepting my fears, assured me of a wonderful ride to our home pastures.

Great was the rejoicing when, five weeks later, we reached

129

Wadi Sirhan. Though thousands of Bedouin tents were staked out, it did not take us long to find the abode of Nuri Sha'lan. Like wild fire, the good news was spread abroad. Groups of women and children on foot, and men on camels and horses joined us from all directions.

Nuri kissed his grandson Fuaz and greeted him, "Thou hast helped to stretch out thy hand against the Shammar and inflict great punishment upon them. Their wealth has been plundered, and great lamentation has risen among our enemies. Indeed, we were in despair about thy absence, but now we exalt the name of God for the delivery from all fear."

2

ONE EVENING, as I was taking Alia and Ghazal to a rain pool for water, a long train of at least three thousand camels trailed along the ridge of a nearby hill. Herdsmen and armed guards, on foot and on horses, tended to the flocks.

These people, we heard, were of Tudmur (Palmyra). They had bought the great flock from the Wuld Ali tribe, now pasturing with the Ruala. The traders of Tudmur and the guardians of the Wuld Ali would drive these animals to Damascus. I rode over to the armed men to inquire about Sheykh Ammer from whose pastures these camels had been brought.

One of the armed guards, a Negro on horseback with his dog following him, left the flock and, yelling at the top of his lungs, raced over to us.

Ghazal reared and pulled on his rope, which slipped from the girth of Alia, for, Bedouin fashion, it was only tucked in. Before I could slide down from my camel to hold on to Ghazal, he bolted away toward the rider.

I watched the Negro dismount, throw his arms around Ghazal's neck, kissing his eyes and forehead, while Ghazal neighed his delight.

The Negro, one of Sheykh Ammer's old slaves, had for years taken care of Ghazal. I saw the fellow was crying and that Ghazal nuzzled the Negro's neck and shoulder.

131

"Thou art, then, Aziz," the Negro said to me. "I bring thee greetings from Sheykh Ammer, who left for Damascus many days ago."

I couched Alia, and the slave and his dog sat down with me to wait for my friends. We talked, leaning our shoulders against an ancient cairn of stones, and the great flock of camels disappeared over a hill.

That night I took leave of Ghazal. I had to accept the fact that he had been only a loan to me, not an outright gift. I recalled to the slave my promise to Sheykh Ammer in Egypt and asked him to ride directly to Damascus with the stallion. In that city he would return Ghazal to Sheykh Ammer and also inform my friend that I would be in Damascus within a few weeks.

"I have chosen," I said with finality. The slave, understanding my insistence, answered, "The Ever-Living God cannot plunder thee of thy hope, and leave thee desolate. God himself will revoke thy decision, for art thou not branded with a burning love for Ghazal? Exult with a full heart even when thy hero is led away. Sheykh Ammer, gentle in his love, will delight thee with a greater joy and restore and recover the led-away."

Life can be a chain of manifestations of the Deity. I felt it when this faithful Negro spoke to me. This devoted man was a bit of this divine spirit which is in every creature. The love for animals may be just another form of our Creator in us. "I possessed" Ghazal. Now I must let him go. But still I held him within me, in the kingdom of spiritual love where all things of beauty and perfection are enshrined forever. And while sitting there in the desert night, I was touched by the peace that flowed from the beautiful spirit of the simple and gentle Negro. And I had hope that I would see Ghazal again.

"How great is the ever-living restoration," the slave assured me as he left, "and how great is Ghazal's splendor to gladden our hearts."

His eyes had followed my gaze upon Ghazal and he said, "I ask leave, Aziz."

We said farewell and I laid my hands upon Ghazal's forehead.

The pride of my life had gone. The wail of my heart sounded within me. "The night and my mare know me," says the Bedouin proverb. My heart knew that night, and Ghazal knew me.

The silvery neigh of Wudiyeh rang out after him through the still night. Ghazal answered her with the reassuring call that he was not far. Later, when Ghazal realized that he was being taken away from her and from me, his scream tore through the dark—a vibrating, heartbreaking call that died away beyond some hill.

That night I lay awake until dawn. I was glad when the sun stood high and the world looked real so that I might try to visualize where, on their way to Damascus, the slave and Ghazal were.

In the meantime our illicit operations in the cultivated land of Mesopotamia had become known to the Turks. Their commander at Dumeyr dispatched an emissary to Nuri's camp, looking for the responsible leader of our raiding party —Rashayd.

But Rashayd could not reconcile his conscience with the prospect of a Turkish dungeon. He lost no time in riding away to the south to assist Nauaf at Jauf. Before we parted, he offered Wudiyeh to me. It was his desire that I keep her and also the foal that she would bring into the world. I hesitated to accept so great a gift, but Fuaz and Mnahi persuaded me to accept Wudiyeh, and Rashayd urged me once more. Perhaps he had sensed that he must leave Wudiyeh behind. "Fear not to take her. She will fill thy soul with splendor and consecrate our memories. Let her spirit stand amongst us forever," he said.

A week after his departure we received the tragic news that Rashayd was killed near Jauf. I think he must have known his death was near, else he would not have consented to being parted from Wudiyeh.

When Fuaz saw the tears well up in my eyes over the loss of our friend, he said, "Let not the cloud of grief tremble in thine eyes. Rashayd has crossed by the passes of the Nufud into the pastures of the moon." These childish words of consolation to alleviate my sorrow were an expression of that primitive faith which all Bedouins have. Whatever befell Rashayd, he would live forever a raider among chivalrous people in heavenly pastures on the moon.

Rainfalls had been abundant. Young shoots covered tamarisk and ghada bushes, and the tracks of oryx and gazelle under every bush betrayed their browsing places. Nuri and his tribe were moving into rich pastures. They urged me to meet other clans and allied tribes which I had never seen before and to look at their horses.

Mnahi guided Fuaz and me across Wadi Sirhan to the edge of the Nufud desert where many of the Ruala camped. Here at the edge of the great Nufud we expected Wudiyeh to foal almost any day now. Mnahi and I took her past the fastnesses of the Tawil, a volcanic range breasting the mountainous dunes of the Nufud. Spring had come! Bright flowers

134

flourished among the rocks; even the camel-thorn bush burst into bloom here, and stunted acacias shed a sweet fragrance. At times our camels and horses were powdered all over with blue and yellow pollen.

This red sand desert of the highland of Nejd was the cradle of the Bedouin race. Wild animals found refuge here, and the Bedouins with their mares and their great flocks of camels retreated to the soft, warm dunes and there found repose. Upon fragrant pasture, under green tamarisks and ghada bushes, new life was born in spring.

Alia, the tender-hearted, became wistful, and her mother instinct worked within her with devastating effect. She investigated every little fuzzy baby camel that peeped out of the tall bunches of Nusi grass, as if it might, by some miracle, be her own. She was hysterically happy when one of these little creatures smelled her or started to lick her. Her stomach then rumbled with excitement; her full-throated belching and the grinding of her teeth expressed supreme contentment.

She had been so fond of Ghazal, but now she became very attached to Wudiyeh, grazing with her leisurely every day in the same pastures, tied to her by Wudiyeh's halter rope.

In the desert, among animals, rare friendships develop. By habit and instinct Alia and Wudiyeh were one family, and I did not have a great deal to say about it. Now that Wudiyeh was expecting her foal, the two seemed to conspire against me.

No longer could I just untie Wudiyeh's halter rope from Alia's saddle girth and ride off alone with my camel. Alia would not move a leg unless we took Wudiyeh along. And if Wudiyeh were too tired for a little journey, I had to call a lad from a nearby tent to care for the two and ride off on some other camel. When I attempted to tie the mare to Alia's girth and let a herdsman take care of them, neither of the animals would budge, for Wudiyeh preferred to be unattached at that moment and to trail behind alone, though not out of sight of Alia.

The withered old desert had miraculously renewed herself, had become beautiful again with the bloom of youth. The gentle caress of rain and sun had touched the cheeks of the wilderness with color. Deeper glowed the green of the flower-strewn meads in the wide depressions. Perfume-laden, the soft spring wind blew over the gracious land.

Throughout the last day Wudiyeh had been wandering toward the red sand dunes that rise so abruptly from the high plateau. No one interfered with her. Guided solely by her own will, we allowed her to move at leisure. Browsing with Alia over the meadows, nibbling yellow-green shoots, Wudiyeh entered the silent world of the sand hills.

Mnahi assured me that Wudiyeh knew her time had come and that she was heading for a warm, sheltered spot in the dunes. Her udder had grown heavy with milk during the last hours.

We rode after her on our camels. The stems of wild herbs rustled faintly as they broke under the pads of Alia. Wudiyeh stepped carefully over long strands of exposed roots of the ghada and tamarisk bushes, halting often to look about her.

The day was clear and still. There had been no dew in the mornings of late. It was an opportune time, Mnahi said, for the angels to descend to Wudiyeh's feet with their gift from heaven. Destructive spirits, he said, descend only with the dew, for it hides them from the sight of men.

136

Mnahi, like all the slaves, was filled with anxiety about omens. As we trailed the mare that sunny afternoon, and I listened to his strange wisdom, I did not betray my lack of faith in his superstitions.

On and on, Wudiyeh led us, lazily, while the sun was declining, and a breeze came from above like the slow beat of wings. The dunes turned a deeper red; the wondrous silence of the Nufud closed in upon us.

As Wudiyeh headed for a wide-spreading acacia in the hollow between two sheltering dunes, a vulture rose from the feathery yellow branches and winged languidly away.

"Ha!" Mnahi cried with loud triumph. "The evil spirit. Allah driveth him off; may He destroy him!" And he shouted to Wudiyeh, "O daughter, hasten after thy luck, for this is a good omen."

Mnahi slipped from his camel and stepped in my path, crying, "Stay thee! Here we camp."

The shadows of night lengthened around us. Wudiyeh lay down under the tree. Mnahi spread a goatskin upon the ground and began his prayers.

I was to stay with Wudiyeh this night, while Mnahi took Alia and his own camel a mile or so away to where members of his family awaited him.

But he warned me, "Earth spirits are guiding the beasts of prey. Sleep thou, Aziz, with only one ear and one eye this night. The jini are fond of drinking warm blood. Behold the vulture has left its perch on the tree to proclaim to the wild beasts of the Nufud that Wudiyeh has taken shelter by the acacia!"

Mnahi left his rifle under my saddle cover. So carefully was the old gun wrapped in rags, that, in a crisis, I could never have made use of it in time.

"Let us trust in God rather," Mnahi said piously, as he rode off with his camel, with Alia trailing behind.

I lay down in my sheepskins and coats, about a hundred paces away from the mare, and slept with "one ear and one eye" as Mnahi had cautioned me, not, however, to surprise the evil spirits, but rather to care for our little mare.

The pale slender crescent of the moon and the morning star hung deep over Jabal Tawil. . . . When I awakened, an eerie dawn glimmered faintly upon the dark waves of the dunes. Beneath the acacia tree, which rose against the dark hill, there was a pale glow. This was the grey of Wudiyeh's coat. She lay quietly, with her head raised; another body, radiating a silvery light, was beside her.

I hastened out of my sheepskins, and walked quickly over to the mare.

"Wudiyeh, ya ruhi—oh my soul!" I called.

She heard my voice, and gave a weak, an utterly weak answer.

The vulture rose swiftly from the acacia tree, bending the slender boughs as his wings brushed through. Every leaf shook, and the yellow pollen floated down like snow to the ground, shedding sweet fragrance upon the mare and upon the transparent, enveloping shroud beside her.

The angels had been there as Mnahi had promised and had left their heavenly gift at Wudiyeh's side. There was life in that silver shroud. Through its beautiful transparency, a pair of black, shining hoofs tore, and a white star on a shield-like forehead emerged.

The foal was out of the shroud now. He gasped for air, gazing with blinking brown eyes upon the world. His ears quivered; his long legs trembled, his gleaming dark coat was all ripples. The tip of his pink tongue stuck out from the side of his mouth in a blessed funny way, and upon his curly iron-grey coat the yellow pollen kept floating down.

Wudiyeh laid her tired head upon the earth and sighed deeply and closed her eyes. From time to time she ground her teeth, and small shivers shook her form. Foam appeared upon her lips; her face was moist, as if she had cried. I stroked her mane and spoke words of consolation to her. She lifted her head, and looked at me with moist, wistful eyes.

The vulture had returned to its perch in the tree above, under which Wudiyeh lay.

I heard Mnahi dismount. He bent down beside me and whispered a prayer of thanks that Wudiyeh's life had been spared again. "Rejoice!" he cried to Wudiyeh. "Though anguish still trembles in thy soul, the jini have not tasted thy blood," and scooping up the sand, he buried the silver shroud.

Now the little foal struggled to his knees and rose upon his swaying hindfeet. He tumbled down, and tried again, bracing himself with his forehead against me, balancing himself with legs wide apart and uttering his first sound. Though it was only a bleat, Wudiyeh heard it and turned her face to him. She saw her own son standing beside her.

With a loud, happy neigh, she answered her baby's bleat. Casting away her own helplessness, she struggled to her feet. Now with a sudden resolution, the wobbly baby creature stepped forward and on tottering feet began to search along his mother's side. When a spray of dripping milk tickled his nostrils, he sneezed, and excitement quivered through his body. Fresh from heavenly pastures, he knew the precious milk of his mother and began to draw it in with deep content.

Exhausted finally, he dropped lazily to earth, his sides

heaving, his silky nostrils still gasping for air. Sleepily, Wudi-yeh looked about her, swishing her tail. Now she stretched her shapely neck to reach for the drooping branches above and began to nibble at young shoots. But when her son stirred, she strained her eyes towards him and nickered. Then she bent down and licked her baby conscientiously again.

Mnahi suggested that we leave the mare and her foal and ride over to fetch Alia. When we returned, I could hardly restrain Alia from rushing headlong down the last slope to the tree where the mare and her foal slept, but suddenly she stopped and her whole body trembled as if she had seen an apparition.

The newborn foal gazed with large eyes upon the gaunt camel and tried to turn away, but his tottering feet got all mixed up and he tripped.

Alia looked at him, whimpering with an expression of utter helplessness. Life was more than she could understand. Deep murmurs rose from her throat as I urged her forward to nudge with her nose at the baby foal.

Before noon of that first day the little fellow had walked at least two miles away from the dune where he had been born, and before the evening of the second day, caprioling around Alia and his mother on our way to Nuri's tent, he had made the complete descent from the sand dunes of the Nufuds to the plain.

Among the sidr trees of the valley a child advanced on a sorrel mare. Behind him rode his bodyguard, mounted on red horses. The men held tall lances on their right hips, and silver chains jangled from the broad blades of their quivering long spears as they approached us.

The young rider was Fuaz. He had seen us return from

the sand hills. At once he spied the little foal and shouted, "Behold a fawn of the Nufud, a large-eyed antelope, a kuhaylat of the antimony skin and the twinkling hoofs!"

"He is a Drinker of the Wind!" Mnahi answered.

"Masha'llah!" the young prince cried excitedly. "God has planted a star upon his forehead. May Nijm be his name!"

Mnahi echoed his plea. "In the name of God, let it be Nijm —the Morning Star!"

Nijm was a lovely foal. His silky silver-grey hair covered his black skin like the heavy down of a fledgling bird. The motions of his spraddling legs, the haughty toss of his head, the proud carriage of his fuzzy tail, endeared him to everyone. His eyes were large and eloquent, and his nostrils like satin, with fiery red veins traced into the black skin. But there was something else about Nijm—something more important to me. He was the son of Ghazal and Wudiyeh, and a living reminder of Marzuki and Rashayd, and of the journey from the Nile to the Euphrates River.

A question formed in my mind. I tried to relate Nijm to that search I had begun in Greece, but I had to admit that Nijm—alas!—was not the horse of my quest. Rather was Nijm very much like any other horse I had discovered in Arabia. Nevertheless, I appreciated the gift of my foal and his emaciated little mother and I wanted to bring them home to my sister in Egypt as antique souvenirs from an ancient and faraway land.

3

SUDDENLY I FELT a desire to leave Arabia. Almost a
year had gone by since I had left Egypt. Perhaps the wither-
ing pastures reminded me that I had lost all sense of time. I
consoled myself with the thought that at least I had migrated
and raided with the Bedouins in their desert wilderness, and
that I could claim that I knew their horses from having lived
among them. But, alas, I had bought none of them, I was
coming home empty-handed. I had not considered one of
their animals worth purchasing for our plantation. What
would Butrus say? I was definitely worried.

The Ruala began to assemble in preparation for their great
trek through the Hamad. Gladly I accepted Nuri's invitation
to join them on their migration to the north, as this would
bring me in a most leisurely fashion back to Damascus.

Nuri regretted that I had not found the horses I came into
the desert to buy. He said, "It entered into thy heart to interest thyself in our horses, but hast thou not hastily concluded to judge over them? The time has elapsed, and thou
hast examined our fair ones. Unfasten thy decision and lead
some of our horses with thee."

I argued. I wanted him to understand that I had come with
a definite purpose in my mind. I described to him the type I
had seen in ancient sculpture. His inconspicuous little horses,

I admitted, had endurance and strength, but they all lacked the points which were essential to me and to the horse breeders in Europe and Egypt.

"The God of Majesty has raised our horses among us in the flesh," Nuri said. "Those images thou hast seen among the Rumi—Greeks—were made of stone and are heathenish. Perfection was with our forefathers in the desert and found favor with us. Hath not the hand of God made all these? And hath not God endowed our horses also with intelligence greater than that of any other creature?"

I agreed.

Nuri said nothing.

While I felt discouraged about the failure of my trip, my mind slipped to Ghazal. Would he know me when I saw him again? He had been my companion as God had intended the horse of Ishmael to be. There was a sinking feeling within me that I had lost Ghazal forever. He was a king of horses—just as father had once told me the Arabians were—and he had a gift of knowledge almost like a man's.

As the migration started, dark clouds hung over us. Mnahi anxiously scanned the horizon, saying that it foretold evil for us, and passing herdsmen urged us to avoid crossing ravines and boulder-strewn washes, or—better still—to wait until the storm was over.

Mnahi and I decided not to try for the shelter of a tent but to stay out in the storm in order not to lose sight of our animals.

The clouds burst open; rain poured down upon us amidst new flashes and blasts of thunder. We were enshrouded in darkness, cut by the groans of camels and the desperate, piercing cries of our herdsmen trying to prevent a stampede.

The wind grew colder, and we were drenched and shivering. A ghostly, milk-white cloud churned above us, moving swiftly with a hollow sound. With a hard, hissing noise, hail stung our faces; it beat the earth and rebounded like bullets. The icy white gravel crunched under the feet of our nervous animals.

Out of the storm the yells of herdsmen came nearer—the high-pitched singing voices trying to reassure the terrified camels. Gaunt shapes bore down upon us. A large herd of camels, wild-eyed and bellowing, galloped with spraddling legs through the slush of mud and hail. Hardly had they vanished when another torrent of stampeding animals poured down from the mountain, sweeping along living boulders of their own kind which had lost their footing. Thousands of them were on a rampage. They closed in upon each other, surging together in the panic which caused the maddened beasts to seek protection among their own kind.

Mnahi knew the danger, knew that we might be drawn into the torrent of animals if we did not leave everything behind—saddles, blankets, covers—and quickly gain higher ground. We prodded little Nijm along and led Wudiyeh, Alia, and Mnahi's race camel to the nearest incline, only about a hundred feet above the gigantic whirlpool of camels.

If we had not held fast to Alia, she would have been lost. As senselessly as a horse runs back into a fire, she strained to rush with her fellows to destruction. Mnahi's race camel was gone before we knew it, gone with the bellowing, pounding herd. We never laid eyes upon her again.

Swiftly as it had come, the storm passed, leaving almost seven hundred dead animals in its wake, most of them in the ravine below; fourteen tents from Nuri's camp were swept away with everything in them except—praise be to Allah!—

144

the children and the women who had fled with their men to a higher spot.

The afternoon sun shone upon a land so thoroughly soaked that it could not have drunk more. Our little family lazily scattered along the slope during the comfortable warm hours of noon. Animals and men rested with dreamy, half-closed eyes. Nijm, not yet addicted to the boring habits of his elders, could not understand why the world around him should suddenly be so dull. He gamboled over to Mnahi's new race camel, frisked about her legs, and bleated softly. She, susceptible creature, gazed intently at the handsome little colt. Minutes passed, and she fell in love with him, with his silky coat, and his saucy manner. Why wasn't her baby like this splendid one? Overcome by her maternal feeling, milk spurted from her udder. The greedy Nijm scented it at once, investigated the source, and began to drink.

The she-camel, wildly happy in the delusion she had brought into the world this beautiful child, closed her eyes, perhaps to dream about this comely being she had acquired. Slowly, rhythmically, she began to chew her cud. . . . Finally she roused herself to look around at him with soft, tearful eyes, to touch him with anxious lips.

A roar arose from Mnahi. "Hai, hai—move on!" he shouted to his camel.

Obediently the foster-mother tried to push Nijm gently away. But the little colt only clung to her with greater fervor and whinnied pleadingly as the perturbed camel moved her legs and dumped the little fellow upon his knees. Nijm looked groggily about him, milk dripping from his nose. He was drunk with sweet camel's milk. He dropped right where he was, and sprawled out to sleep just as the rest of us had been doing.

Wudiyeh, now fully awake, beheld her son from afar. For a time she watched him maternally, too relaxed to move. But when she saw his tender hide twitch and his legs strike out in sleep, she, wise mother, knew that insects were bothering him. She moved slowly over to her son, blowing gently upon him to drive the little pests away. Nijm slept in her shadow then, and the silky hair of Wudiyeh's shortened tail swept across his tiny form as she watched him out of the corner of her eye.

Mnahi still grumbled at the mother camel. When I asked him why, he said, "All camels are stupid and ugly. Their tragedy is that they know it, but their comfort is that they may blame the horse for it."

"The horse?" I asked. "Blame the horse for their ugliness and dull manners?"

Mnahi's eyes had closed again, and his answer was only an indifferent "Hah" to my question. He was half asleep, but he had aroused my curiosity, and I wanted to know the story.

I begged him again, but not until I had dug out our coffee-pots from his camel saddlebag—his one weakness was for that bitter brew—did he tell me the story.

"Sometime after God had given the mare of the Angel Gabriel to Ishmael," Mnahi said, "the little mare complained to Him of many things. 'My back is chafed,' she cried. 'I desire a soft but solid object on my back, and a longer neck, the better to reach the pasture. And I long for the split hoof of the antelope, that I may move more easily through the sand of the desert.' But God hesitated to change this beautiful animal, for she was a Drinker of the Wind, handsome of line,

146

made for swallowing the earth. God thought deeply for many days, asking Himself: why, if creation were perfect, should He alter it?

"Instead of changing the mare, He created the camel with a long neck and cloven hoofs and a hump to be the burden carrier.

"The mare was terrified at the sight of this stupid, ugly-looking beast and tried to run away. But God stayed her, saying, 'Have I not granted you your desire?'

"The horse admitted her ingratitude and asked to be forgiven.

"God is just," Mnahi continued, "He does not change His perfect creatures.

"And God decreed that the camel should forever be a companion to the beautiful mare, to remind her always of her ingratitude and her willfulness.

"The camel—aware of her ugly form—looks forever wistfully at her handsome companion. And this is the reason," Mnahi concluded, "why my camel fell in love with little Nijm, trying to delude herself that he was her son—her sleek, humpless son, a Drinker of the Wind."

Everyone prophesied that Nijm would be an unusual colt —as clever as his father and as gentle as his mother, hardy and swift. He galloped with us every day. Often I wondered how many thousands of miles a young horse covered in the first year of life in Arabia. The Ruala migrated easily three thousand miles within a year. Their horses, going back and forth between camps and pastures, must have covered at least twenty miles a day.

Nijm grew rapidly into the most amusing creature on four legs. He followed Wudiyeh, clumsily trying to imitate his mother's ways. Her attitude was one of tolerance, but the manner in which she looked out for her baby betrayed her secret pride in him.

In those days Wudiyeh began to share my moods, my joys, and my sorrows. When I laughed with my companions, Wudiyeh neighed as if joining in the humor of our conversation. She grew quiet when I was sad or tired. If I saw her head hang pensively, I could blame only myself.

Explaining the mystery of such a relationship, Mnahi said to me, "To the degree that an Asil—highborn horse—possesses thy heart, will she respond to thee. She will humble thy enemies and honor thy friends. Willingly she will carry thee upon her back, but she will consent to no humiliation. She is at once aware whether she carrieth a friend or an enemy of God. The mare that lives under divine orders as a mute and obedient companion of man, has an insight into the mind of her master whom she may even prefer to her own kind."

As Mnahi explained these things to me, I began to understand the close friendship between the desert man and his horse.

4

NURI AND I, IN the company of retainers and slaves, had left the Ruala in the Hamad desert. We rode through the pastures of the shepherd-hills toward Damascus. But with each step that brought me nearer to the end of my journey the bitterness of my disappointment over the failure of my quest for the ideal horse increased. Empty-handed I must go back to Egypt and admit frustration to Butrus and Charlotte. The thought sickened me and brought on a depressed mood, but Nuri knew how to dispel it and restore me to my good humor. He said that after all I had satisfied myself and gained the knowledge I had always wanted to gather of the history and breeding of the Arabian horse.

As we rode across the pass of Jabal Ruak toward the plain of Dumayr, the sun flamed red behind a bank of menacing clouds, but Mt. Hermon's silvery-white peak rose clearly beyond Damascus. The sky over the desert quivered with lightning, the thunder rolled and echoed from the rocks. A little stream of water ran along the side of the road. Abruptly it stopped. The fragrance of cultivated land rose to our nostrils. Rain swept the distant hills, and blue smoke drifted from adobe huts.

Nuri swung his riding wand and his high-legged mount went into longer strides.

"Nuri," I cried.

He looked back and waved his arm with a gesture for me to follow him, but I had dismounted. We were leaving the desert and I wished to take farewell of it. Here the herbage was thick and tall, the ground covered with flowers. Across the pass I looked back to the desert and the wind blew to my nostrils the dry air of the wilderness. I spread out my arms as if to embrace it. I looked up to see if my little friend with the speckled breast would be around to bid me farewell with his rapturous song. But only thunder shook the air. Once again I felt the loneliness as my gaze swept beyond the grasslands into the desert. I stood in silent gratitude while my friends went on. Then I remounted and rode after them through the green glades, deeper into the winding plain toward a village where we all assembled to spend the night.

Nuri chatted gaily as we rode next day along the snow-waters of the Barada River, past olive orchards and walnut groves. Even the solemn Mnahi grinned at my eagerness to see Damascus again. Lush green fields and walled-in gardens with stately trees surrounded the suburbs. The roads were filled with peasants bringing their produce to town on burden camels, donkeys, and horses. Their foals trotted behind them. We made slow progress as we entered the native quarters, but Mnahi led us through the whole city, through the crowded bazaars to the spacious Maidan. There among the cultivated gardens and the mud walls of the Damascenes we rode up to the pale blue gate of an old adobe house, severe and lovely as the earth of which it was built. Tall poplars shaded the flat roof; a primitive mosque with spindly leaning minaret adjoined the house.

We entered the great inner court and, as we rode into it on our tall camels, like true chieftains of the desert, a robed man walked toward us. He was frail with a pointed beard and a thin face. He wore a checkered red and white kaffiyeh with a plain black aghal, and a reddish-brown shepherd coat. There was a great gentleness upon his face and no haste in his walk.

It was Marzuki! In an instant I was out of Alia's saddle, my arms thrown around my friend.

"We have grown in grace," he said slyly. "We ought to thank God for allowing thee to return alive. Before setting out again to face the desert, we may pause and well consider the dangers you may have to meet."

Nuri's weathered face was puckish with good humor when he rejoined us. He bade me follow him and Marzuki. Entering a second yard, we faced an open stable. Marzuki's nephew and two other men greeted us. Twenty horses stood about in the enclosure along the wall. They were magnificent, well-groomed animals with glistening coats, well fed and in perfect condition.

I was aghast!

The truth slowly dawned upon my mind. The shock of the beauty of these creatures was followed by the realization that they had once been the same poor, shabby, disheveled horses which I, in my ignorance, had discarded in Nuri's camp and among the tribes of the inner desert. Here were the creatures in whom strength and beauty blended in perfection, whose proud carriage and handsome shape were indeed like that of the horses of Phidias. Their eyes flashed with fiery light, their nostrils flared defiance, they tossed their heads upon lofty necks.

I was silenced before the beauty of this sight. Defeated and helpless I looked at Nuri. Amused, he watched me, funny little wrinkles creasing his face.

"I have been deeply concerned with thy vain search among us for good horses," he said. "When I noticed that thou couldst not find a single horse fit to purchase from our tribe, I allied my faith with thy mission in the desert. I asked Marzuki to bring my own horses with him to Damascus while thou wast engaged far away on the great raid. Thy grief be dispelled; success shall grow from the ground like grass under thy feet. Where now are the blemishes of our horses? Faded as by the breath of the sun!"

I could not find words to thank him. Nuri had saved me. With a gesture of his hand he waved away my words of gratitude.

"I have only one request to make of thee," he said. "I shall ask thee to sell my horses to Butrus, thy Egyptian overlord."

No Bedouin would ever be so willing to sell his mares; he will not part easily with them for money. It could only be that Nuri had prepared this sacrifice to save me.

"My horses shall eat thy bread," Nuri continued, "until thou art filled with remorse, and until thou art willing to declare before witnesses that our Drinkers of the Wind, the pride and wealth of the Bedu, are the animals thou hast been looking for."

I felt humiliated in my blindness but at the same time so overjoyed that for the moment I could not answer. When I at last found words to speak and rebuke myself for my ignorance, Nuri said very gently, "Let us thank God for His cheerful gift of such animals to us."

One by one Nuri's horses were led out into the green meadow. They challenged me; they looked defiantly at me who had denied them in the wilderness. Indeed, they were like the horses of Thessaly. They were the creatures of my quest.

Nuri singled out a three-year-old colt. This young stallion was a grey. Not even in sculpture had I seen a finer head. His profile boasted an extreme concave indenture, and his enormous eyes were like those of an antelope. Seen in profile they were almost in the center of his head.

This colt was of the *antique* type of horse that my intuition had always felt existed: the horse with the pyramidical shape of the head, the concave facial profile, the diagonal cut of the flaring nostrils, the small firm lower lip, the great width between the eyes, the wide-set jowls, the disc-like jawbones, and the bulging forehead.

I had known him long before I ever went into the desert—when I stood under the frieze of the Parthenon.

I had found a model that might have belonged to Phidias.

I had found the quivering-limbed steed with the glistening coat of my childhood.

From the other end of the stables I heard Nuri shout as the slaves returned the horses to their stalls.

"God who girds my strength and measures my strides, let Him be my witness that Aziz may choose one of two things —sixteen of my horses against his little family of two."

I shook my head. Nuri cried, "Reflect on thy answer before thou speakest."

"I have chosen, Ya Amir," I answered him.

". . . *or* this perfect blue-grey colt against Nijm?"

Again I shook my head.

"Once," I said, "thy slave had only one sense of sight, a very confused one, but now thy servant sees and knows the truth."

Nuri understood me. He knew I had learned that my own

two horses, under their starved, rough, unkept condition, were as beautiful and perfect as his own.

I thought of Ghazal, who with proper care and feeding would have looked just as magnificent. I realized that I had possessed all the time the *antique* horse but had never recognized it. To Nuri I confessed my feelings. "Ghazal," I said, "was indeed the horse I was looking for and a companion to me from God. He was as beautiful as any of thine . . ."

"To expiate thy mistakes," Nuri interrupted me, "Sheykh Ammer has contrived to assail thy heart with gladness and joy."

Concealing further words under his tongue, Nuri took my arm and walked with me to the garden back of the yard and stables. We entered the deep recess of a vaulted entrance to an adobe house. A curtain separated the women's part of the house from the mejlis of the men. From habit I wanted to pass the place, for an Arab never shows curiosity near the seclusion of women. Perhaps someone might be asleep behind the privacy of the curtain—but Nuri urged me on.

I heard a gentle neigh. My feet stopped, for I knew this voice.

"Oh, God, let it be Ghazal!" I cried.

I rushed forward and parted the cloth. My eyes beheld a horse—a golden chestnut with a star on his forehead, and four white feet!

With steel shackles still clanking upon his pasterns, Ghazal stumbled toward me. As if by a magnetic power, he was being drawn to me, but suddenly he stood still and regarded me with startled eyes. Did he not know me? Gazing upon me hesitatingly, he switched his tail and twitched his ears.

"Ghazal," I cried, moving closer to him. He tossed his head eagerly, reached toward me to bury his nostrils into my

154

left armpit and inhaled deeply. It was the old gesture of love and a sign of his surrender.

Tingling with excitement and happiness, I touched his muzzle and his forehead. It was the same muzzle and the same forehead of my beloved Ghazal, but it seemed a new Ghazal, a shining, perfect, beautiful one. Well-groomed and fed, noble and handsome, proud and virile—I stroked his mane, his powerful neck, his broad golden back, felt his muscles and tried to press my hand into the rock-rounded flesh of his croup. I raised an armful of the luxuriant, silky hair of his tail and held it against my cheek. The sense of his beauty and perfection stirred in me a profound emotion—a love compounded of happiness and pain. It made me hope, suddenly and deeply, that in a life beyond life there might be Ghazal.

I had no doubt that I had found the horse of my quest. His head with its gazelle profile was fairly short. As he tossed it up and down and neighed in high spirits, playing with the bright-colored tassels of his halter, his mouth, with its small, firm lower lip, revealed teeth of gleaming ivory. His large, thin, wide-open nostrils were like petal tips of a rose or like delicate pink shells. Above the dark fire of his eyes, with their long, shining black lashes, rose high and shieldlike the bold, expressive forehead bearing the silvery-white star. His head was wide between the jaws and had the afnas, a concave indenture of the whole nasal bone, whereby distinguished ancestry is recognized. The curve of the windpipe culminated in a wonderfully arched throat. The contour of the neck resembled an elongated wave, from which floated in brilliant ripples the silken mane. His small, straight, inward-pointing ears quivered like "lilies trembling in flowing water." His whole body swayed, lithe and slender with supple strength.

His breast was deep and majestic, and his sloping shoulders had the characteristic "swimming motion." His back, short, wide and distinctly seamed, was ideal for the saddle. The muscles of the level croup were strong, the secret of his ability to "soar" and "poise," as the Bedouin says. The tail of fine hair, carried high in perfect arch, had grown again, tapering at the tip. His thighs, like those of an ostrich, were muscular; his legs light, but cleanly modeled and firm, with elastic pasterns, long and strong, and hoofs as hard as rock. He was of flawless proportions and balance. His short, fine, silky coat shone like a mirror.

Looking at him now in his perfect condition, I understood why Al-Buraq, who carried the Prophet to Paradise, and Rukhsh, the famous charger of Rustem, were called "the gleaming horses."

I was so absorbed that I had not noticed a child and a Negro who had entered. It was Fuaz, and it was obvious that something moved him deeply. Looking up through his tears, he said to me in a gentle voice, "How sweet for thee to greet thy gazelle, the leader of the herd."

In his right hand he was holding something which the slave urged him to give to me. Bashfully he extended his hand. It was a date stone and a pebble. Fuaz said, "By these tokens it is well to remember our brotherhood and Ghazal, the horse of thy youth, a hero who took our shadows away."

These last were the words Nuri had taught the child on that evening in the desert when the old chief had dropped his gold-embroidered shepherd coat at the feet of Ghazal.

Then the old Negro, the same slave to whom I had entrusted Ghazal in the desert, took the newly grown strand of hair which was hanging over Ghazal's forehead and straightened it out. With his dagger, the slave cut off one kurun (lovelock) from Fuaz's crown of hair and carefully braided it in one single plait into the forelock of the stallion. "The angels of God," the slave said, "descend by night and visit our horses, laying their hand on the nauwas—sacred forelock —and bless the animal and his master."

Then the slave gave me a message from his master, Sheykh Ammer, who had gone back to Egypt and the Libyan desert to visit his relatives. Standing very straight, the slave recited, " 'Hail to thee, Aziz.' Thus hath spoken Ammer, my uncle, 'Give praise to God that our gazelle hath been restored to us. Now we return him to our brother, and to our son, Aziz. Hail, we smell the fragrance of sweet memories in the pastures of el-Hamad and en-Nufud. There we shall meet again, and never shall we be pursued by the specter of want.' Thus hath spoken Ammer, my uncle. 'May Ghazal have his fill and allay his thirst; may he dwell in a manor that riseth high above the horizon to bid us welcome from afar; and may he dwell under the luster of the stars and the full moon.' "

The old slave placed the key to Ghazal's shackles in my hand, and taking Nuri and Fuaz as witnesses, he said, " 'To produce evidence,' so sayeth my uncle, 'let there be this pair of shackles and this key to be lifted from Ghazal, and let the dark-skinned one with the star upon his forehead be the property of Aziz as we have decreed.' "

In this manner did Sheykh Ammer make Ghazal his permanent gift to me.

During the week following my arrival in Damascus, I had to attend to a number of details concerning Nuri's horses. From the Turkish Telegraph Office I wired Charlotte the news of my arrival and of the success of my journey. She replied that all was well and that Butrus, the manager of the plantation, was leaving within a day to meet me in Damascus.

Butrus arrived as announced, and with efficiency and without sentiment took the business end of my journey into his hands.

He bought Nuri's horses, paying a fair price—thirty-four hundred gold pounds for sixteen horses—and resold them at once at a great profit to people in Syria and Egypt. Even the magnificent grey colt was disposed of. He fetched the highest price—seven hundred pieces of Turkish gold.

I felt heartsick to let these magnificent horses go—the perfect grey colt in particular—but I could not have kept him myself. The price asked was beyond my means. I consoled myself that I had lived to see the perfection and beauty of these horses and had succeeded in my quest, and I gave thanks to Nuri, whom I had learned to love and respect like a father, for this supreme moment of my life.

Butrus wanted me to return immediately to the desert to visit other tribes, but I persuaded him to let me have a vacation in Egypt with my sister. So, while Alia and my horses were being loaded on the train for Palestine, Marzuki treated us to a farewell dinner at his house. We sat at tables, and not on the ground as at other times. Nuri's slaves, who were serving, encountered some difficulty getting around the unaccustomed chairs and passing an unbelievable number of cups, plates, and bowls containing choice vegetables, small morsels of meat and fish, and various kinds of sweets. Nuri touched very little of the "city-fare," as he called it, and asked Mnahi to bring a goatskin and pour out some sour milk into a huge wooden bowl. He drank and handed the vessel to me, saying, "Aziz, this is the day of delight and the time to renew my covenant with thee. Wherever thy path will lead thee and wherever the earth smiles and makes room for thee, remember us."

Marzuki rose and said, "Let us recall to mind that God is our friend, Who ever directs our feet from the wasteland to cheerful pastures and from sunstricken rocks to rippling pools of rain."

Thus the eloquence of my friends found expression in poetic language. Each one spoke in his own way of deep sentiment regarding our friendship.

Mnahi had come in and he reported to Nuri that the horses were loaded and that the train would leave very soon. "Let Aziz not return alone, as if in flight," he begged Nuri. "Let me guard his life and the vessels of his joy. Loosen the ropes from my neck, my uncle. Let me be free to march with Aziz and watch over him with my eyes."

"Rise, and go with Aziz," Nuri cried.

We had taken leave of our friends. Damascus and the desert were far behind us. Swiftly the train bore Alia and my horses towards Haifa. Mnahi was supremely happy to see the outer world. He said to me, "The hills are a roof of green grass and flowers, and the sea a shining face, sweeping away my longing for the desert."

My first view of the great expanse of the Mediterranean through the eyelids of a beautiful dawn brought me back at once to my life in Egypt.

At Haifa, Mnahi and I placed our animals in strong shipping crates and hoisted them onto the boat for Egypt. Two days later we landed in Alexandria.

Charlotte's voice was choked with tears as she took my arm and said, "Never again do you go to the desert without me."

I took her hand and led her down to the lower deck. "But

159

look," I cried, pointing to our horses, Ghazal, Wudiyeh, and Nijm. "The gifts that have increased with our faith!"

Ghazal looked at Charlotte with his soft meditating eyes. Perhaps he did recognize her. Charlotte climbed on the shipping box and laid her hand upon Ghazal's neck and felt his satin coat. The stallion liked her touch. His ears quivered; he champed his teeth, neighed loudly, and tossed his little head.

Charlotte was mysterious about something, and finally admitted that she had a surprise waiting for me—a new home in Ramleh. The place to which she took me contained two acres of land. It overlooked the ocean just above the palisades, where the ancient Greeks had buried their heroes and where Ghazal once had carried me into the roaring tide.

"There," Charlotte said, pointing, "we can ride along the beach as far as Montazah . . ."

Date palms shaded our bungalow with their heavy bundles of fruit and wide crowns of ribbed leaves. A few paces away from the low wall surrounding our garden, a solitary black goathair tent stood at the foot of a large sand dune.

Marzuki, Charlotte said, had sent this spacious tent as a present to us. He knew that Charlotte and I, who loved the desert and the dwellers in the tents, would want the illusion of vagabondage.

Charlotte and I remained all night with our horses under the black curtain of Marzuki's tent. We watched the morning star as it paled over the desert, and within me memories rose like the waters of the great river.

We had found our world beyond the hills.